SOCIAL HISTORY OF ASSAM

By the Same Author:-

- Development of Administration in Assam with Special Reference to Land Revenue-Justice and Police 1874-1920
- History of Arunachl Pradesh
- Social and Cultural History of Ancient India *(Revised and Enlarged Edition)*

About the Author

Dr. M.L. Bose, is Reader in History, Dibrugarh University, where he has been teaching since 1967. He took his Masters of Arts in History and his doctorate from Jadavpur University. He has presented and published more than a score of papers in different Seminars and Conferences and learned journals. His earlier publications British Policy in the North East Frontier Agency and Historical and Constitutional Documents of North East India (both by Concept, 1979) and Development of Administration in Assam (Concept 1985) made his name known to a wide reading public.

SOCIAL HISTORY OF ASSAM

Being a study of the origins of ethnic identity and social tension during the British period 1905-1947.

M.L. BOSE

CONCEPT PUBLISHING COMPANY, NEW DELHI-110059

ISBN 81-7022-224-9

First Published 1989
Reprinted 2003

Published and Printed by
Ashok Kumar Mittal
Concept Publishing Company
A/15-16, Commercial Block, Mohan Garden,
NEW DELHI-110059

Phones : 25351460, 25351794
Fax : 091-11-25357103
Email : publishing@conceptpub.com

Contents

Dedicated to the Students

of

Dibrugarh University

Prologue

On the publication of a summary of this book in the *Journal of Historical Research*, Dibrugarh University, in July 1978, a serious tension was created in both the campus of Dibrugarh University and Dibrugarh town. Meetings were organized by all sections of the University community and public meetings were arranged in the town. the circulation of the article was stopped and the distributed copies were called back. Gradually the tension spread all over the State when news was published in the newspapers. A social tension was created by the article which had only tried to analyse the causes of tension in the British period.

Much of the tension, probably the entire situation, was due to rumours spread by some persons who had read the article but who did not have historical knowledge and understanding of the matter. The rumour had offended the sentiment of many people who were led to believe that the author of the article had tried to malign the Assamese people and created disharmony among different communities. Not only that, the author was believed to have tried to prove the numerical minority of the Assamese people in the State and to have held the Ahoms responsible for many social evils in the Brahmaputra valley. The rumours were reinforced by the withdrawal of the article from circulation, and an appeal to the Assam Sahitya Sabha for redress by some teachers of a Department of the University. An emergency meeting of the Teachers' Association of the University condemned the author without examining the context of the article, and requested the authorities to call back the original report from the Indian Council of Historical Research on the alleged ground that it contained many distorted facts, and asked the author to return the money he had received from the I.C.H.R. for the Project.

The University authorities, under pressure of circumstances and insistence of some members of the Executive Council, had no alternative but to ask the author and the Editor of the Journal not to resume duties after reopening of University on the charge of academic indiscipline and called for an explanation from the author why proceedings should not be initiated against him for writing the article containing "gross distortion of facts" with a view to creating communal discord.

When the University debarred the author and the Editor from joining the duties, the matter was reported in the newspapers from Delhi, and editorials supporting the author started appearing in the *Times of India, Economic and Political Weekly, Mainstream, Radical Humanist*, etc. as also in the local press. There was clear appreciation of the authors treatment of the subject and the allegations against him were dismissed as baseless. Then came a wave of all-India protests against the action of Dibrugarh University by teachers of different Universities of the country and by the Indian History Congress, Indian Council of Historical Research, Indian Council of Social Science Research, Centre for Studies in Social Sciences, Calcutta, and many such organizations. The Chairman, University Grants Commission, expressed concern over the issue and the Chancellor of the University called information from the University on the proceedings of the matter.

In the meetings at Dibrugarh, in course of discussions, to avoid tension it became clear to many that it was not the author who had tried to create a social tension but some people had seized the issue to create disturbances in the state. Thanks to the sagacity of the students of Dibrugarh University and its teachers, the tension was defused by the distribution of xerox copies of the original report which practically killed the mischievous rumours and restored to some extent the reputation of the author which some interested people had tried to undermine by malicious and false propaganda.

The Teachers' Association of Dibrugarh University now changed its stand on the issue. A new idea and principle of "academic freedom" now gained popularity and people held that if the article at all contained any aspersion on Assamese society, the author should have the academic freedom to write what he considered correct.

The publication of this report in the form of a book, it is hoped, will remove all misunderstanding regarding the article. In fact its publication was suggested long back during the wave of trouble over the article by one of my well-meaning friends. But as the situation was very tense in Assam at that time I did not like to go ahead with the idea and, moreover, I was under an obligation to the I.C.H.R. whose permission was necessary for publication in the present form. Now that the situation has been eased through the untiring efforts of the peace-loving citizens, and members of the University, I take the opportunity to publish the book and place the same before the reading public.

A word must be said about the book to keep the record straight. I have not altered the contents of the report, though I feel the work needs to be done in depth. But in the book I have put the references at the foot of every page to provide for the reader a ready reference to the sources of information. Re-arrangement of the first three chapters has been done, changing the original structure of the report submitted to the I.C.H.R. to make the book a little more systematic.

Dibrugarh

March 31, 1986.M.L.Bose

Acknowledgements

I am grateful to Swami Bangobinda Parampanthi who kindly loaned me a typewriter for typing out my work, and our Librarian-in-charge, Mrs. S. Das, who very kindly provided books for completing the references.

ONE

Introduction

A paper of research type was prepared by the author and was presented in a Seminar organized in the Department of History of the Dibrugarh University sometime in April 1973. The paper was well received, and subsequently published in a research journal SHODHAK issued from Jaipur, Rajasthan, in 1973, and was reprinted in the Journal of the Assam Political Science Association in 1974.

The original paper entitled "The genesis of Ethnic Identity and Social Tension in North-East India" had emphasized the social and cultural unity of the north-eastern people and had taken a stand that before the advent of the British, there was no social or communal distrust in North-East India and there was no linguistic problem, no communal riot ever took place, nay, there was no ethnic or race consciousness among the people of the region; separative and mutually opposing and hostile race or ethnic consciousness and factional feelings began to germinate and raise their ugly heads only during the British regime as a result of the systematic persistent propaganda and encouragement given by the Anglo-Indian Administrators and scholars alike.

The paper tried to analyse the data found in some government reports and publications, following the usual Indian tradition of putting all blame on the British Administrators and scholars for everything bad in Indian life, and prove that ethnic consciousness and communal rivalries had resulted from systematic attempts to sow the seeds of discord by the imperialists. The general acceptance of the paper in all quarters and ready acceptance of it as a basis for further investigation into the subject by the Indian Council of Historical Research, New Delhi (ICHR) by providing funds prove that it was quite in tune with the thinking of the scholars of the time.

Be that as it may, the project director proposed to study the origins of race consciousness and separate social and linguistic consciousness among the people of North-Eastern India during the British Period, especially of the period 1905-1947, on the basis of literary and archival sources. North-East India which is the erstwhile State of Assam had been a political unit of the British Indian Empire where several socio-cultural and linguistic groups and tribes were administered for over a century and thus gave these diverse communities a unique chance to live together in a spirit of mutual understanding and cooperation to the British rule. But the "divide-and-rule" policy of the British Government was also applied to Assam and the Administrators fostered divisive tendencies and encouraged factionalism in the region. The result was that communalism, factionalism, race antagonism began to divide the society into segments.

SOURCES

From the last quarter of the 19th century the different ethnic groups and social groups began to be organized. These organizations focussed their especial problems and suggested their origin and solutions through memoranda, pamphlets and other publications. In the annual meetings and conferences of special groups and communal organizations, printed lectures and addresses of their leaders were distributed. For example, the Ahoms of Assam formed an association in 1893, published memoranda and lectures and through their leaders tried to establish their separate identity as a minority and secure redress of their grievances. The Assam Association similarly made organized efforts to protect the interests of Assam. The Assam Sahitya Sabha, through its publication, tried to rouse Assamese nationalism and the Muslim League and many tribal organizations distributed leaflets and pamphlets to propagate their special and particular identity and interests. The Government sometimes appointed committees to investigate particular problems and the reports of these committees highlighted the warring interests of several groups. The Assam Administrative Reports and Census reports emphasized the divisiveness in society. The debates in the Assam Legislative Assembly sometimes spread communal tensions. Some leaders published booklets to catch the attention of the people. Local magazines and newspapers published articles which pointed out peculiar interests of different people. These provide ample material of study to understand the attitude and origin of the divisive organizations and their spirit.

No attempt has so far been made to study the origins of these consciousness and social tension in the area from an academic point of view. The Government of Assam had appointed a committee after the disturbance of 1960 to report on the language problem, and the findings tried to only correlate the factors of disturbance in the post-independence period. Therefore, the necessity to study the origins of the problems by a study of the above mentioned sources in the British period which prepared the ground for the post-independent partition of Assam into a mosaic of North Eastern Council, remained.

SCHEME OF STUDY

The project proposed to (i) study the political developments in North-East India, i.e. Assam, (ii) draw a picture of pre-British socio-cultural conditions in Assam; (iii) study the growth of population in the modern province of Assam, (iv) study the dynamics of social and cultural change and draw a socio-cultural profile of modern Assam and (v) to trace the origins of ethnic identity and social tension in the new environment.

THE PROCEDURE FOLLOWED--METHOD OF STUDY

The project having been sanctioned by the ICHR the project director started the investigation into the subject in depth. As there was no provision for an investigator or assistant in the project, the director had to carry on the work single-handed. For the collection of data on the topic, the director, therefore, planned to visit the State Central Libraries of Assam and Meghalaya in the first phase and side by side explore the archives of the above States in Gauhati and

Shillong. Subsequently tours to Calcutta were undertaken for a study in the National Library, West Bengal Secretariat Library and West Bengal State Archives. Finally, the National Archives in Delhi was visited. The tours were undertaken either availing leave from the University or during the Puja and summer vacations. (The project director expresses his gratitude to the immediate past and present Vice-Chancellors of Dibrugarh University for allowing him to avail leave without prejudice to his teaching assignments). It should be mentioned that long gaps in between tours made it a little difficult to pursue the study with sustained energy and action.

The methodology followed was the usual historical method of studying or rather scanning, books, journals, pamphlets and newspapers in the different libraries and exploration of the archival materials related to the subject matter. The Census of India Reports of the year 1874-76 to 1941 and Secret Police reports together with Government proceedings particularly were surveyed to collect relevant data for the study. The shifting of the capital of Assam to Gauhati from Shillong made it a little difficult to collect all relevant information from all the departmental proceedings preserved in the Assam Archives as many papers could not be had for consultation. However the best possible use was made of the material available.

TWO

Physical Geography

PHYSICAL CONTOUR

The erstwhile State of Assam which may be called North-East India lay within 28° 15" 24° latitudes and 89' 46" 97°4" longitudes.[1] But it presents a complex of physical features : hills and dales, swamps and forests, vales and meadows. Yet they can be conveniently divided into two broad divisions: Plains and Hills. The districts of Goalpara, Kamrup, Darrang, Nowgong, Sibsagar and Lakhimpur (now divided into Lakhimpur and Dibrugarh districts) along with Cacher and Sylhet formed the plains Division while the Garo Hills, Khasi and Jaintia Hills (which is now known as the State of Meghalaya), North Cachar and Mikir Hills, Mizo Hills (now known as Mizoram) and Naga Hills (now known as Nagaland) came under the Hills Division. Besides, the North-East Frontier Tracts now known as Arunachal Pradesh formed parts of Assam, and Manipur Political Agency remained under the charge of the Assam Administration. [2]

The valley of Brahmaputra is a long alluvial plain, about 450 miles long, and of an average width of 50 miles.[3] Shut in by mountains on the north-east and south, with the Brahmaputra flowing through its entire length from east to west, and crossed by countless tributary streams of every magnitude, falling into the central channel from the bordering mountains on either side. The uniform level of the valley is intersected by a few low conical hills, projecting like spurs. The converging hills at Goalpara appear almost to shut in the

Assam Valley, and may be called the Gate of Assam. The low-lying tracts on both sides of the river throughout the valley are subject to innundation for a width ordinarily of about six miles on each side of the stream; beyond that distance the level rises gradually above the reach of the higher flood.[4]

One of the principal characteristics of the Brahmaputra, attributable perhaps to the large amount of silt brought down by it, is its tendency to change its course.[5] In the Assam valley its encroachments, though at times of considerable extent, are limited by the hills; but the deviations of its lower course have been most remarkable.

The valley of Surma comprises the two districts of Sylhet and Cachar. It is intersected by the Surma or the Barak river. On the north the valley is shut in by the Khasi and Jaintia hills, and the Naga hills; on the east by the Manipur hills which form the watershed dividing the water system of eastern Bengal from that of Irrawaddy; on the south lie the Lushai and Tipperah hills.[6]

The western and eastern portions of the Surma valley differ considerably in their physical features. The western portion, comprising the district of Sylhet, is for the most part a large alluvial plain, averaging some 70 miles in width, with clusters of low sandy hillocks, locally termed "Tilas", scattered here and there[7]. It is traversed by numerous streams and watercourses, running principally from west to east, whose margins in many cases are somewhat more elevated than the surrounding country. Consequently during the rainy months of the year, from about June to October, the whole of the district with the exception of the hillocks and the villages built on the elevated banks of the river, or artificially raised, is under water[8]. In the south, however, the country becomes somewhat hilly, being penetrated by several spurs running out from the higher ranges in Hill Tipperah. In the centre of the district, a detached range of hills crop up and is called the "Ita Hills"[9]. All these hills are covered with dense jungles.

In its eastern portion consisting of the district of Cachar, the valley narrows, and presents very diversified features. Low detached spurs and offshoots from the main hilly tracts which bend the valley on both north and south extend, covered mostly with dense jungle, almost to the river's edge on either side, with rich alluvial valleys between them[10]. Most of the low lands in these valleys remain under water during the rains.

The Surma or Barak river rises among the chain of mountains to the north of Manipur. After flowing for about 180 miles through a mountainous country, it becomes navigable for boats of burden about 20 miles above Banskandi, a village in Cachar, and, passing across that district, divides into two branches at Bariga, the eastern limit of Sylhet district"[11]. One branch flows nearly due west, by the town of Sylhet and Chhatock, and falls ultimately into the Megna. The second branch called Kasiara flows diagonally across the Sylhet district in a south western direction, and reunites with the northern branch near Lakki, about 26 miles above its junction with the Megna[12].

The Naga Hills, Khasi and Jaintia Hills, and Garo Hills are a continuation of the mountainous chain which sweeps round the head of the Brahmaputra valley. Each range has marked physical features of its own[13].

In the north-eastern parts, in the neighbourhood of Jeypur, the Naga hills consist of small broken ranges running generally northeast and southwest or long irregular spurs leading down into the plains, usually steep on the northern side, with a more gradual slope on the south[14]. The intervening valleys are very narrow. The major portion of the whole tract remains uncultivated, and covered with dense jungle undergrowth. In the higher hills there is cultivation on the southern faces. Further westwards, the hills are more rugged and abrupt. The main ridge, named the Barrail, in the neighbourhood of Samaguting, is remarkably precipitous in character, and towers to the height of 10,000 ft[15]. On the western slope of this ridge a good deal of terraced rice cultivation is carried on by the Nagas. In other parts the cultivation appears to be exceedingly sparse.

The peculiar feature of the Khasi and Jaintia range of hills is the abruptness with which they rise almost perpendicularly from the Surma valley on their southern face, attaining rapidly an altitude of over 4,000 ft; while on the north side the ascent from the Assam valley is characterized by a succession of gradual spurs and detached ridges[16]. The lower portions of these hills on both sides are clothed in dense forest and jungle. The upper plateau and main central tracts consist of a succession of undulating downs, broken here and there by the deep valleys of the large hill streams, and crossed mostly with short grass, having been completely denuded of forest by the migratory cultivation of the inhabitants, except where a few sacred groves have escaped the general devastation. Shillong, which is situated about the centre of this tract, stands at an elevation of 4,900 ft, while the ridge overlooking it, the highest of any part of the range, is 6,449 ft above the sea[17].

The Garo hills, the termination of this chain, present very similar characteristics, being steep and precipitous on the southern face, and sloping in gradual ridge to the plains on the northern and western sides. They are of rather lower general elevation; the highest peak of the range, below which Tura, the Headquarters of the districts is situated, being not more than 4,700 ft. above sea level[18]. Tura itself has an elevation of only 1,300 ft.

The lands in Assam may be divided into three great classes[19]. The first division consists of the mountains and hill ranges which again may be subdivided into three sections, the great mountains chains; independent group of hills; isolated hills and hillocks. The second class consists of hills lying in groups, large and small, on the plains of the Brahmaputra valley, and forming either independent units by themselves or continuations of the northern or southern ranges. The largest group is that of the Mikir hills. The third division of the land is what may be called "the alluvial plain of the valley, its level being generally above the ordinary innundation of the Brahmaputra and of its tributaries".

The soil of Assam greatly varies in character. The greater part of the territory west of the Sankosh river consists of a mixed free soil, which is ash colour and singularly uniform in character, and is composed of light friable loam, superimposed on a deep bed of pure sand. The soil of the Brahmaputra valley, though varied, is on the whole exceedingly fertile, and well adapted to all kinds of agricultural purposes. "For the most part it is composed of a rich black loam, reposing on a grey sandy clay, though occasionally consisting of a yellow clayish texture"[20].

In Sylhet, the soil is, for the most part, bluish clay, which becomes black on the borders of the "bils" or "hoars". The low isolated hillocks, or "tilas" are composed of soft sandstone. In Cachar the soil of the plain is alluvial deposit of sandy soil[21]. The several groups of hills situated in the valley are of granite formation, the granite containing frequently veins of quartz. The surface soil of these hills is a rich sandy loam, while the surface soil of the hillocks and moulds of the districts of Sylhet and Cachar is of a rich vegetable mould [22].

The climate of the province of Assam, both in the Brahmaputra and Surma valley, is noted for its extreme humidity. Besides continuous rain in season which commences in March and ends in October, occasional showers occur.[23] At Cherrapoonjee, which is situated at the south edge of the Khasi hills, immediately overlooking the plains of Sylhet, the rainfall is famous for its excessive amount (500 inches per annum).[24]

The Brahmaputra valley enjoys a far more equable temperature than is generally found throughout India, the warm weather being very moderate and nights throughout the year cool and refreshing. Yet its climate has always been far from salubrious.[25]

Throughout the province earthquakes are very common, both in the plains and in the hills.

NOTES

1. *An Account of Assam and its Administration* p. 1.
2. *Report on the Administration of Assam 1874-76.*
3. *Report on the Administration of Eastern Bengal and Assam 1905-06.*
4. Ibid.
5. *Assam Administration Report 1874-76.*
6. Ibid.
7. Ibid.
8. Ibid.
9. Ibid.
10. Ibid.
11. Ibid.
12. Ibid.
13. Ibid.
14. Ibid.

15. Ibid.
16. Ibid.
17. Ibid.
18. Ibid.
19. Ibid.
20. Ibid.
21. Ibid.
22. Ibid.
23. Ibid.
24. Ibid.
25. Ibid.

THREE

Formation of the Province of Assam Under the British

The beginning of the new State of Assam goes back to the year 1826 when, on February 22, the British compelled the Burmese to accept the Treaty of Yandabu, though Goalpara and Sylhet had already been acquired by the East India Company in 1765 when they obtained the Dewany of Bengal Suba from the Mughal Emperor Shah Alam.[1] Assam was held by the British as a conquered territory.

After the expulsion of the Burmese from Assam D. Scott made two alternative suggestions: first, the Brahmaputra valley should be restored to an Ahom prince who should pay subsidy; second, the area as far as Biswanath should be annexed to Bengal, the upper portion of the province should be restored to an Ahom Prince providing for proper arrangements for the defence of the Assam-Burma Frontier.[2] But the Supreme Government ordered for the annexation of the entire province. But Scott held tenaciously to the idea of restoring an Ahom prince in Upper Assam and as such developed a plan of administration, the principle of which was to make as little alteration in the existing institutions as possible in Upper Assam while thoroughgoing changes were proposed for Lower Assam.[3] In 1835 the territory of Lower Assam was divided into three districts of Kamrup, Darrang and Nowgong.[4]

Meanwhile the feasibility of restoring Upper Assam to an Ahom prince continued to be discussed. At last on June 27, 1833, on the recommendation of Robertson, successor of D. Scott, Purandar

Singh was placed in charge of Upper Assam when he agreed to pay an annual tribute.[5] The Government of Purandar Singh, however, proved unsatisfactory to the British. Within three years he began to default in payment and begged for reduction of his tribute. He was pensioned off and the territories under him were placed under direct administration of the British Officers in October, 1838, and the territory was divided into two districts of Sibsagar and Lakhimpur.[6] The system of administration devised for the lower valley was extended to this area.

Cachar was originally ruled by an independent native dynasty before the first Anglo-Burmese War.[7] It was invaded by the Burmese, whose assistance was sought by some of the disputants for the throne of Manipur. Govinda Chandra, the Raja of Cachar, applied for British help and, in 1826, a British force expelled the Burmese from both Cachar and Manipur.[8] On conclusion of peace in 1826, Cachar was restored to Govinda Chandra who agreed to pay tribute acknowledging the Company's sovereignty.[9] But he failed to subjugate Tularam Senapati who carved out for himself a tract which was bounded by the Mahur river and the Naga Hills on the south, the Doyang on the west, the Dhansiri on the east and on the north by Jamuna and Doyang rivers. In 1830, when Govinda Chandra died issueless, Tularam laid claim to his territory on an anterior pedigree. But, according to the terms of the treaty of 1826, Govinda Chandra's tract was formed into an independent district under the charge of a British superintendent in August, 1832.[10] Tularam was given a pension of Rs. 50 per month. He was deprived of the title of Raja and the right to administration of justice except in tribal cases. Subsequently in 1853, the rest of Cachar was added to the British territories."[11]

Matak, the tract south of Sadiya, was given to a Chief called Bar Senapati, who had protected its people from Burmese atrocities, on condition of supplying "paiks" which was later converted into a monetary payment. The Bar Senapati died in 1839, nominating his son Maju Gohain but the latter refused the new terms offered to him whereupon the tract was annexed to the British territories.[12] In 1842, by a formal proclamation, Matak and Sadiya were incorporated into the British territories and were subsequently added to the Lakhimpur District, the headquarters of which was transferred to Dibrugarh in the Matak country.[13]

Sadiya was placed under a Khamti Chief who swore fealty to the English. But in 1835, a dispute arose between the Sadiya Khowa Gohain and Bar Senapati regarding a tract of land. The political agent at Sadiya attached the land in question and called the disputants to appear before him to prove their claims. The new Sadiya Khowa Gohain forcibly occupied the land without appearing before the Political Agent. Thereupon the post of Sadiya Khowa Gohain was abolished and Sadiya was placed under British control.[14] The Khamtis, however, were exempted from taxation and were allowed to manage their tribal affairs but their control over the Assamese people was abolished.[15]

While these developments were taking place, the local officers of the semi-independent tribal tracts of Khasi Jaintia hills found it necessary to bring these tracts under immediate British control. Nunklow, in the Khasi hills, had been adopted as a place of residence by some European British subjects in 1826 under a treaty with the Raja who had agreed to allow a road to be constructed across the Hills to connect Cachar and Sylhet with the Assam Valley. Some officers engaged in the construction of the road were massacred owing to a misunderstanding in 1829. Troops were called up for reprisal and in January 1833, Tirat Singh surrendered himself to the Company. A political agent was appointed for general superintendence over the Khasi and Jaintia hills.[16]

Meanwhile in 1832, four British subjects were seized by Raja of Gobha, a vassal of Jaintia King. Three of them were immolated at the shrine of Goddess Kali and one escaped to tell the tragedy of his fellows.[17] At this juncture, Ram Singh died and his successor, Rajendra Singh, declined to make over the culprits to the British. Thereupon the Political Agent, by a proclamation, annexed the Jaintia parganas to British territories and added them to Sylhet. A few weeks later Gobha was similarly annexed to Nowgong. But the Hills remained under the Political Agent at Jowai and the Raja was pensioned off.[18]

Three Thanas of Goalpara, Dhubri and Karaibari originally formed part of the district of Rangpur of Bengal. By regulation X of

1822, they were separated from the Rangpur district and exempted from the operation of General Regulations and subjected to a special system of Government along with the Garo hills.[19] The new tract was called North East Rangpur and David Scott was appointed the first Civil Commissioner to administer it. When Assam came under the East India Company in 1826, this tract was placed under the charge of the new administration of Assam.[20] But in 1867, the Koch Behar Commissionership was formed and then North-East Rangpur and Eastern Duars which was obtained from the Bhutias in 1866 were made parts of this new Commissionership.[21] In the following year judicial administration of the Garo hills and Goalpara was placed under the Judicial Commissioner of Assam, but the executive control remained in the hands of the Commissioner of Koch Behar.[22] Finally in 1874, when Assam was made a separate Administration, Goalpara and Eastern Duars were transferred to Assam.[23]

The Garo hills were included in the district of Goalpara till the year 1866. In that year a special Civil Commissioner was appointed at Goalpara for these hills. But the measure proved a failure and an officer was posted at Tura in the Garo hills. This action proved satisfactory and the matter was then regularized by the Act XXII of 1869.[24]

Besides these districts Assam Administration had to deal with numerous warlike tribes who surrounded north, east and south of Assam Valley. Many of them laid claims to rights more or less definite over lands lying in the plains; others claimed tributary payments from the villages below their hills or services of the villagers. The British after annexation of the province had to treat them fairly and liberally. At the beginning they were anxious to leave the tribes alone and paid them cash commuting their rights and dues from the villages.[25]

But unrestricted intercourse with the tribes by the British subjects caused misunderstanding and quarrels with the tribes and sometimes expeditions had to be sent to punish the guilty tribes. Therefore Bengal Frontier Regulation V of 1873 was provided for drawing of an Inner Line travel beyond which was restricted.[26] In 1880, after Assam was constituted into a Chief Commissioner's province in 1874, Assam Frontier Tract Regulation was issued to provide for the removal of certain enactment from the frontier tracts inhabited by these tribes.[27] This was supplemented by another Regulation issued in 1884.[28]

These wide tracts were divided by a Government of India Notification into three sections in 1914, e.g. (1) The Central and Eastern Tracts; (2) Lakhimpur Frontier Tract; and (3) Western Section. The first and third were placed under the charge of Political Officers while the second was put under the charge of the Deputy Commissioner of Lakhimpur District.[29] The Headquarters of the Central Tract and Eastern Tract was located at Sadiya and of the Western at Charduar. In 1919 the Central and Eastern Tracts were renamed as Sadiya Frontier Tract and Balipara Frontier Tract.[30]

This Frontier Tract was reconstituted in 1943 when certain portions of Sadiya Frontier Tract and Lakhimpur Frontier Tract were formed into Tirap Frontier Tract with headquarters at Margherita by Eastern Frontier Tract Regulation (Internal Administrative).[31] This new unit was placed under a Political Officer. In 1946 again Balipara Frontier Tract was subdivided into Sela-Sub Agency and Subarnasiri Sub-Agency.[32] In 1948 Sadiya Tract was bifurcated into two charges of Abor hills and Mishmi hills.[33]

The tribes of Naga hills who are numerous and speak different dialects called by distinctive names are collectively known as Nagas. The British Government did not like to bring under their immediate administration the unproductive hill tracts inhabited by these turbulent tribes. The policy followed at the beginning was to hedge them in within the hills and non-interference in their own affairs and close the neighbouring markets in case of misdemeanon. But the chronic atrocities perpetrated by the Angamis forced the British to station an officer at Asalu in 1854 and a line of frontier posts was established. This measure having failed in 1866 Angami country was formed into a district with headquarters at Samaguting which was subsequently moved to Kohima in 1878.[34] The policy now followed was a penetration and the incorporation of other places. In 1875, Lotha Naga and in 1889. Ao tracts were annexed and in 1917 Kuki tracts were added to the district.[35]

Lushai hills stretched from south-east of Assam to Chittagong.

The southern tracts were inhabited by the Kukis. Later on the Lushais became masters of the hills and the Kukis were driven to the northern fringes. In 1860, the Bengal Government passed Act XXII to adopt an administration for the Bengal portion of the Kuki hills which were in constant ferment.[36] The north Lushai hills in Assam being a constant source of trouble, political officers were posted at Aijal and Lungleh in the nineties. The Government of India proposed the amalgamation of the two portions of the hills in 1893 and it was effected in 1898 when the entire hills were placed under a superintendent for general administration and transferred to Assam.[37]

The inconvenience of administering such a diverse country as Assam consisting of 10 districts as an appanage of Bengal was keenly felt in the 1860, and the issue of separation of Assam from Bengal was opened for discussion.[38] Meanwhile a comprehensive report on Assam was submitted by A.J.M. Mill in 1854 and a Memorandum on the North-East Frontiers of Bengal was prepared by Sir Alexander Mackenzie in 1864.[39] It was revealed that a diverse country like Assam having peculiar problems of its own and occupying an important strategic position and possessing unexplored potentialities could not be effectively administered as an appanage of Bengal.

Indeed, the administration of Bengal had become unwieldy. All the additions to British territory in northern India right from the North-Western Frontier to the Salwin were practically under its control. Besides the superintendence over the administration of the presidencies of Bombay and Madras was vested in it. Possibility of a fourth Presidency for the government of these vast territories was also mooted. Therefore the Act of 1853 provided for constitution of Lt.-Governorship. A Lt- Governorship was created in Bengal in 1854 to relieve the Governor-General from the administration of Bengal. But this did not solve the problem of the administration of Bengal. The Governor-General was no doubt relieved of the burden of the Bengal administration and now could engage himself in all-India affairs exclusively.[40] But the problems of administering a huge territory under a Lt.-Governor was more keenly felt now. In the then system of government there was no vestige of local-self government and the administration had to look after every aspect of human life besides rendering general duties of administration. Besides Government by a single man was most inexpedient and dangerous. Therefore, the Act of 1854 had provided for the creation, by proclamation, of local administration, with prior sanction of the Board of Control and the Courts of Directors, in any part of India to provide for the administration of these territories particularly which might not be advisable to include in any Presidency or Lt.-Governorship.

But in Assam repeated revolts of the tribal population in the frontier and the unprecedented havoc of the famine of 1866-67 in Bengal highlighted the snags in the Bengal administration. The necessity of separation of Assam from Bengal was now to be considered. George Campbell, the Lt.-Governor of Bengal, wrote: "No doubt whatever that separation of Assam and the Eastern Frontier, or any other large province would be an advantage" even though he tried to prevent the separation of Assam from Bengal. He, of course, desired to keep Bengal intact, but at the same time he wanted to keep Assam as a special Commissionership. The Secretary of State for India had, as early as April, 1871, agreed upon the proposal to make Assam a separate charge under the Government of India.[41] He wrote, "I cannot doubt that, when strength and directness of power are required in any subordinate administration, it is best to place that administration immediately under the Supreme Government, so that it may, as directly as possible, enjoy the suppport, and carry authority, of the Governor-General in Council. Assam and eastern districts seem to be eminently a case requiring such an administration".[42]

In fact Assam was at that time a very backward country. Bulk of its population comprised hosts of primitive tribes who were unfit for any form of settled government. Only along the Brahmaputra valley the Assamese people had settled life. Yet they could hardly live under a highly developed system of government as was existing in Bengal at that time. Therefore, the Governor-General-in-Council finally determined to take over the existing establishment of the Commissioner of Assam and turn that into a Non-Regulation Commission with a little addition of territory to that to make the unit sizable and economic under a Chief Commissioner.[43]

Originally Campbell had proposed to separate Hill Tipperah and Chittagong districts of Chittagong Division for inclusion into the proposed Commission for their analogous character and importance. But the Government of India considered such inclusion inexpedient. Possibility of transfer of Western Dooars, Cooch-Behar, Jalpaiguree and Darjeeling districts from Bengal to the new province was also considered. But the peculiarity of the problems of the region deterred the Government from such a step.[44]

The territories proposed to be included into the new Commission were the five districts of Assam proper, viz. Kamrup, Nowgong, Darrang, Sibsagar and Lakhimpur, and Naga hills, Khasi and Jaintia hills, Garo hills and Goalpara of Cooch-Behar Division, and Cachar and Sylhet of Dacca Division. The total area was estimated to be 54,000 sq. miles; the population 14,150,000; Revenue was estimated to be Rs. 52.5 lakhs.[45]

The people of Sylhet submitted a memorial against the transfer of the district to Assam mainly on the grounds of deregularization of their district which might result in the abrogation of the jurisdiction of the High Court of Judicature at Calcutta and the substitution of the system of government of Lt.-Governor by a Chief Commissioner.[46] The Secretary of State for India also at first declined the inclusion of Sylhet which formed part of the Dewani Suba of Bengal, Behar and Orissa. But the Government of India persisted in their project of transfer of the district on the grounds that this was not going to alter either the principle or the practice of administration.

From Assam also at first a contemporary news weekly *Assam Mihir* protested against the formation of the new province.[47] It apprehended that the new provincial exchequer might tax heavily the poor inhabitants to meet the administrative charges and abolition of the jurisdiction of the High Court over the Province. But when Campbell pointed out that with a view to giving more attention to the language problem and facilities to the Assamese people the new province was going to be created the paper gave a call to the people to welcome the project. It is interesting to note that a Bengal weekly *Sahachar* had welcomed the idea of separation of Assam much earlier.[48]

Having obtained the sanction of the Secretary of State after repeated telegrams, the Government of India acquired authority, by legislation, to take over from the Lt.-Governor of Bengal, under its immediate authority and management the districts of Kamrup, Nowgong, Darrang, Sibsagar, Lakhimpur, Khasi and Jaintia hills, Naga hills, Garo hills, Cachar and Goalpara by proclamation on February 6, 1874, and on February 9, 1974, these districts, by another notification, were formed into Chief Commissionership[49] and Keatings was appointed Chief Commissioner[49] On September 12, 1874, Sylhet was attached to the Assam Administration.[50] Since Assam was made a Chief Commissionership in 1874 territorial jurisdiction of Assam remained the same till 1898 when South Lushai hills were transferred to Assam.[51]

EASTERN BENGAL AND ASSAM (1905 - 1911)

Though Assam was separated from Bengal the territorial jurisdiction of Presidency had grown unwieldy with the addition of Bihar, Orissa, Chota Nagapur. And though a Legislative Council had been provided for, the charge of administration was too heavy for a single man.[52] The traditional policy of non-intervention was abandoned since the failure of Sir C. Beadon to cope with the Orissa famine of 1866 and projects of reform which transformed the character of administration were introduced in the administration. The Road Cess Act, the Census of India Act 1872, the establishment of Native Civil Service, the extension of the Sub-divisional system, the promotion of primary education, the collection of statistics of all kinds involved a change-over from the *laissez faire* policy to the policy of active intervention for the protection of the poorer classes of society. The growth of population, the emerging importance of the city of Calcutta, the second city of the Empire, the demand for progress in all directions, the important measures of administrative developments which required constant attention, the increasing congestion of business in the Bengal Secretariat,– all these made increasing calls upon the time and energy of the Lt.-Governor.[53] "It is beyond dispute", observed Lord Curzon in his speech at Dacca on February 15, 1904, "that Bengal must be relieved. No one Government and no administration can possibly devote to nearly 80 millions of people the personal supervision, care and control which are the objects for which local governments exist. The interests of the people must suffer and they do suffer....No other local government in India administers much more than half the number of the people that there are in Bengal and there is nothing in the circumstances of Bengal which renders government easier or an exception more defensible here. On the contrary the reverse is, if anything, the case.[54]

Indeed the need for relieving Bengal administration was overdue. As early as 1860 Sir George Campbell had suggested that a Council of Executive Officers should be created to help the Lt.-Governor and the plan was approved by Sir Henry Durand and Sir John Stratchey. But the plan was rejected on the ground that the officers would not be in a position to dispose of business independently; that there would be waste of time as meetings would be irregular and absence of members would entail unnecessary delay; that there would be a lack of continuity; and that the project would increase the labour of the Lt.Governor who could otherwise dispose of business any time he met his officers. But the burden did not decrease and in 1871-72 Sir Campbell observed that the two Civil Secretaries were more than Secretaries, as if they were Ministers of the Departments. Actually they were so. Four years later Sir A. Beadon had to appoint a third Secretary for the finances.[55]

The question of giving relief to Bengal was again raised in 1898 in connection with the proposed transfer of the Lushai Hills to Assam and four years later the whole question of territorial redistribution was taken up by the Government of Lord Curzon.[56] The publication of the proposed redistribution raised a storm of opposition and immense public criticism. On March 18, 1904, in a public meeting the suggestion to create an Executive Council in Bengal and separation of non-Bengali population from Bengal was suggested.[57] It was in fact a revival of the old suggestion of 1867-68 which proposed an Executive Council for Bengal.

But Lord Curzon in an elaborate explanation emphasized the inexpediency of providing an Executive Council to Lt.-Governor of Bengal. Executive Council was necessary for guiding the Governors of the Presidencies of Bombay and Madras who came fresh from England without any experience of Indian affairs. But in Bengal it was sure to create dissension among the Councillors and that would make the administration stagnant and impotent. Because the experts would differ in every respect, and further division of authority would result in weakness and irresponsibility for lack of the focus of authority. The Bengal Council might come into conflict with the Council of the Supreme Government which would be prejudicial for administration. Also the creation of an orderly and efficient government in Bengal would perpetuate the evils from which the administration of Assam suffered arresting the development of the province. Finally experience showed that personal government, not the highly developed form of Council Government, was best suited for the Indian Administration which demanded a well-defined source of authority.[58]

He also ruled out the alternatives with logic. It was suggested by both official and public men that Bengal could be relieved by the separation of the Hindi-speaking tracts and Orissa from Bengal and creating Chief Commissionership in those territories; and Assam could be enlarged, if at all by transferring Chittagong division to that province as suggested in 1898. Curzon opined that transfer of Chittagong would take away from Bengal some best districts and would thus make Bengal universally unpopular while the creation of Chief Commissionership of Orissa and Bihar would make those administrations dependent on neighbouring provinces for borrowing officers. Again Assam would not be self-sufficient in officers and further development both territorial and administrative of Assam would be arrested. And finally the influence of Calcutta over the people of Bengal would remain as it was and that was an unhealthy system of public organization which should better have several centres of public opinion.[59]

The Government of India proposed the reconstitution of Bengal and the creation of a new State to be called North-Eastern Provinces by providing Chittagong Division, Cooch Behar Commissionership and Dacca Division to Assam together with Rajshahi to Assam with the exception of Darjeeling and addition of Malda from Bengal thus providing 31 million people to the new administration while retaining 54 million for Bengal. The new province would have a well-defined boundary continuous throughout its length with well-recognized geographical and social distinction. For a part of its length division between Bengali and Hindi languages would have distinction corresponding with certain physical, linguistic and ethnological characteristics. The new province would bring under one administration the typical Muhammadans of Bengal and provide the city of Dacca a natural capital for such an aggregation. Moreover, the greater part of lands which produced jute and the whole of tea-producing areas with the exception of Darjeeling which had its own characteristics would be thus included in one province. Finally the scheme did not involve the breaking up of commissioners' divisions.[60]

The storm of opposition was ably met with by the Supreme Government. They held that much of the opposition was due to wreckless allegations against tenancy rights and permanent settlement rights. The fear of the loss of national unity of Bengalis was baseless as national unity transcends political boundaries as the Chamber of Commerce did in trade and commerce. As for the loss of rights and privileges, it was pointed out that the new province would be provided with a Legislative Council and in the absence of a Land Revenue Board the Financial Commissioner would be provided which would resemble the implementation of the proposal of Lord Lawrence. The High Court of Calcutta's jurisdiction would remain till a new one could be constituted in the new province.[61]

As for the questions of backwardness of Assam, language, employment opportunity and commerce were concerned it was argued that Assam would benefit by the substitution of Chief Commissionership by a developed form of administration like Lt.-Governorship: Bengali language would not suffer as in the new province the dominating position would be held by the Bengali language: Social and educational aspects were not affected by administrative divisions; employment in the new province would be monopolized by the Bengalis; and finally commerce would take to natural commercial laws and would not suffer.[62]

Public criticism raised some financial objections as well. It was pointed out that the cost of administration of 78 million people would become double with the creation of a new province as 280 more civilians would be required by the new administration, and the new building required by the new province would entail more expenditure. The transfer of papers to the new province would create confusions and some might be lost as well as in 1874. The despatch to the Secretary of State stated that separate reconstitution would, indeed, involve expenditure but that would be met by the revision of provincial settlement from the Government of India's fund and the amount of Rs. 8.5 lakhs was worth paying for the inestimable benefit to be had by relieving the evils of congestion of works in Bengal and arrested development of the province of Assam.[63]

It seems from the above developments that the only thing to which the Supreme Government paid attention was administrative convenience and political considerations. The linguistic, cultural, racial, social or ethnic consideration of the people involved in the issue did not distract them at all. Particularly the interests of the Assamese people and their language were sacrificed at the altar of administrative necessity. People of Assam, of course, were divided in their opinion regarding the addition of territories to Assam but in general there was unanimity regarding the undesirability of the inclusion of Bengal districts of Dacca and Mymensing consisting of an advanced people like the Bengalis whose impersonal form of administration was not suitable for the Assamese who required the parental care of a personal administration.

The objections of the people of Bengal had been refuted by providing the same forms of administration under which they were living.[64]

Ultimately, however, on September 1, 1905, by a proclamation issued by the Government of India the tracts commonly known as North and East Bengal comprising the districts of Dacca, Chittagong and Rajshahi Commissionership with the exception of Darjeeling and addition of Malda were separated from Bengal and together with the Chief Commissionership of Assam was formed into a new Province to be known as Eastern Bengal and Assam and placed under a Lt.-Governor who was to be aided by a Legislative Council and Board of Revenue and over which the jurisdiction of the High Court of Calcutta was to remain as it was in both criminal and civil suits. The Act of 1905 left intact laws which were in force in the areas transferred from Bengal into the new province. The new state was to come into existence on September 16, 1905.[65]

RESTORATION OF THE CHIEF COMMISSIONERSHIP

At the Coronation Durbar in Delhi in 1911, the partition of Bengal was at last declared to be annulled and the Chief Commissionership to be restored in Assam. In fact before the Durbar took place, the Government of India and the Secretary of State had by correspondence finalized the restoration issue.[66] The Government of India wrote to the Secretary of State that the creation of the Chief Commissionership would be reversion to the policy of Sir John Lawrence in 1867. "This part of India (Assam) is still in backward condition and more fit for administration by a Chief Commissioner than a more highly developed form of government." Moreover, "as matters now stand, the Bengalis can never exercise in either province that influence to which they consider themselves entitled by reason of their numbers, wealth and culture". And "anxious as we are to take Bengali feeling into account", the partition must be annulled. The Secretary of State agreed to the proposal and communicated to the Government of India that the Chief Commissionership of Assam should be revived.[67] Therefore the Governor-General in Council in exercise of the powers conferred by Section 3 of the Government of India Act 1854 (17 & 18 vict. c. 77), having the sanction and approbation of the Secretary of State for India by proclamation restored the Chief Commissionership of Assam in 1912.[68]

ASSAM BECOMES A PROVINCE OF BRITISH EMPIRE OF INDIA, 1921

Assam was made a Governor's Province in 1921 when Monteford reforms were introduced under the Government of India Act 1919, and when the British left India in 1947 Assam was one of the seven Provinces of the British Empire of India.

NOTES

1. *Political Conciliations,* March 3, 1825.
2. Ibid.
3. Ibid.
4. *Assam Administration Report, 1874-76.*
5. Ibid.
6. Ibid.
7. Ibid.
8. Ibid.
9. Ibid.
10. Ibid.

11. Ibid.
12. E. Gaih-*A History of Assam*, p.34
13. Ibid.
14. R. M. Lahiri, *Annexation of Assam*, p. 208.
15. Ibid.
16. *Assam Administration Report.* (1874-76).
17. Ibid.
18. Ibid.
19. Ibid.
20. Ibid.
21. Ibid.
22. Ibid.
23. Ibid.
24. Ibid.
25. M.A. Mackenzie, *A History of the Relations the Government*
26. Bose M.L. *British Policy on the North Eastern Frontier Agency,* pp. 156-57
27. Ibid.
28. Ibid.
29. R. Reid, History of the Frontier Areas Bordering Assam from 1883-1941,
30. Ibid.
31. M. L. Bose, British Policy
32. Ibid.
33. Ibid.
34. B.C. Chakrabarti *British relations with the Hill Tribes of Assam* p.20
35. Ibid.
36. Ibid.
37. Ibid.
38. *Proceedings the Home Dep. (public),* October, 1873.
39. Mackenzie, Memorandum
40. Proceedings of the Home Public Dept., Govt. of India, No. 517-33, October, 1873.
41. Ibid.
42. Ibid.
43. Ibid.
44. Ibid.
45. Ibid.
46. Ibid.
47. *Abstracts of Intelligence Reports, Assam police, 1874-1905.*
48. Ibid.
49. *Assam Administration Report, 1874-76*
50. Ibid.
51. *Eastern Bengal and Assam Administration Report, 1905-06*
52. *Proceedings of the Home Public Dept.*, Govt. of India. NO. 155-166, February, 1905.
53. Ibid.
54. Ibid.
55. Ibid.
56. Ibid.
57. Ibid.
58. Ibid.
59. Ibid.
60. Ibid.
61. Ibid.

62. Ibid.
63. Ibid.
64. Ibid.
65. Ibid.
66. *Proceedings of the Govt. of India* (Foreign and Secret) Nos 3-4, August 1911.
67. Ibid.
68. *Foreign Proceedings*. Govt. Of India, June, 1912, Nos. 17-22.

FOUR

Pre-British History and Society

The history of the pre-historic and proto-historic periods of Assam is shrowded in mystery and very little is known about this period. *The Mahabharata, Vishnupurana, Kalika Purana* and *Yoginitantra* indicate that in the early period it was known as Pragjyotisha and later as Kamarupa and was ruled by Kings who had appellation of *Danaba-Asura* which suggest their non-Aryan origin.[1]

The earliest historic record is found in the account of the Chinese pilgrim Hiuen-Tsang, who visited Kamarupa in 640 A.D. It was a strong and prosperous kingdom ruled by a Hindu king named Bhaskar Varman. Hiuen-Tsang places the circumference of the kingdom at 10,000 lee from which Winningham infers that it must have included, at that time, the whole of the Brahmaputra valley, Coch-Behar and Bhutan.[2]

After Hiuen-Tsang's visit again the history of Kamarupa becomes obscure and the veil is lifted by a dynasty founded by Pralambha about the year 800 A.D. The new dynasty ruled for about 200 years when it gave way to the Palas about 1000 A.D. Ratna Pala was the most noted sovereign of this dynasty. The fall of the Pala power ushered in a period of darkness. After a century and a half Pala dynesty was brought under the Pala dynasty of Bengal by Ram Pala.[3]

In the 13th century a new kingdom known as Kamatapura comprising a small portion of the kingdom of Kamarupa came into existence. East of the river Manas and west of the river Sankosh there was still a small kingdom called Kamarupa which owed allegience to Kamatapura[4]. East of this kingdom the territories were ruled over by 12 Bhuyans or Chiefs who had divided among them the valley of the Brahmaputra[5]

The establishment of Muslim power in Bengal affected the course of the history of Assam considerably. While Assam became a constant prey of the Muhammadan invasions from Bengal, the Ahoms made their way into Assam early in the 13th century across the Patkai range[6]. Still early in the 15th century Kamata history attained importance under the Khen dynasty[7]. Though the last king of this dynasty, Nilambor, was overthrown by Sultan Alauddin Hussain Shah of Bengal about the end of the 15th century[8], a new dynasty of Koches was established by one Biswa Singh.

The Koches launched a systematic warfare against the Ahoms for territorial expansion. During the latter part of the reign of king Nara-Narayan, the most powerful and glorious king of the dynasty, a division was made in the kingdom with the river Sankosh as the boundary between them. The old line continued to rule with Koch-Behar as its capital but their kingdom did not include any territory which now comprises Assam. The new branch of the Koch dynasty with their headquarters at Baruagarh ruled over the kingdom which came to be known as Kamarupa. The territory of this kingdom was gradually absorbed by the Ahoms when the last powerful king of the dynasty, Parikshit, was carried off to Delhi by the Muhammadans[9].

The coming of the Ahoms is a decisive factor in the history of Assam. The Ahoms, a Shan tribe, wandered into the Brahamputra valley from Burma about the year 1226. Once established firmly in the Upper Brahamputra valley they followed a policy of expansion and by 1700 A.D. had conquered the territories once included in the kingdom of Kamarupa. About the year 1655 reigning king Chatumla adopted Hindu religion and assumed the name Jaiyadhaja Singh. Towards the end of his reign occurred the first Mahammadan invasion of Ahom Kingdom[10]. Mir Zumla, the Mughal Subedar of Bengal, invaded the Assam Valley in 1662. The accounts of the struggle that ensued are conflicting, but it is certain that shortly afterwards the Muslim army evacuated Assam and Assam did not become a part of the Mughal Empire. In 1695 Rudra Singh , the greatest of Ahom princes, ascended the throne and he completed the conquest of the whole Brahmaputra valley. In 1780, Gourinath succeeded to the throne. His reign was marked chiefly by the rising of the Moamarias which shook the foundations of the Ahom kingdom. Gourinath in utter distress applied for help to the British who had by this time firmly established themselves in Bengal, Bihar and Orissa. Cornwallis sent Captain Welsh with a detachment which succeeded in suppressing the Moamaria rebellion and defeated Kisen Narayan, the king of Old Darrang who had arrogated to himself the sovereignty of the province[11]. In 1809, Chandra Kanta Singh succeeded to the throne and during his reign the Burmese for the first time intervened in the internal affairs of the Ahom kingdom. Chandra Kant having quarrelled with his minister applied for help to the Burmese. Bura-Gohain after the retirement of the Burmese deposed Chandra kanta and set up Purandar Singh on the throne[12]. Third time Chandra Kanta sought Burmese help but at last quarrelled with them who then expelled him and Chandra Kanta fled to Goalpara for seeking British assistance[13].

The Anglo-Burmese relations meanwhile had come to a crisis at that time due to Burmese pretensions over Chittagong, Murshidabad and Burdwan and the English refusal to surrender the fugitives from Burmese territories. Thereupon the Burmese expelled the British from the Sahapuri island, off Chittagong shore. The Government of Amherst on March 5th 1824, declared war on the Burmese[14].

A British force, advancing through the Brahmaputra with a gunboat Flotilla, drove out the Burmese who had mean while occupied Assam as far as Kaliabor; during the next cold season the entire valley came under the possession. Meanwhile the British army in Burma itself advanced upon Prome, the capital of Lower Burma. At Yandabu, General Campbell having defeated, the Burmese dictated the terms of a treaty on September 24,1826, by which the Burmese, inter alia, pledged to abstain from interference of any kind in Assam, Cachar and Jaintia, and recognized Manipur as an independent State[15].

PRE-BRITISH ASSAMESE SOCIETY

Ethnic Composition

If America is the melting pot of the world, Assam can be regarded as the crucible of India. Here not only fusion of races took place from the dawn of human civilization, even today a bewildering variety of racial types and ethnic groups are being forged into a unique type unknown in world history. Both anthropometry and ethnography indicate that most of the early inhabitants of Assam had an admixture of different racial strains, e.g. Negrito, Autro-Asiatic, Mongolian and Nordic[16]. When the first three mingled is unknown to us, but Sanskrit texts lead us to believe that the Nordic/penetration into Assam had begun right from the pre-historic period.

A great bulk of Assam's population of both the hills and plains consist of people of Southern Mongolian stock who are referred to as Kiratas in Sanskrit literature. The hills of Assam, such as Khashi-jaintia hills, Naga hills, Manipur, Mikir hills, Cachar and Garo hills, are occupied by them and some have settled over the plains of the Brahmaputra valley. "With the exception of Khasi which is the only surviving language of the early settlers of Assam, the numerous non-Aryan dialects of Assam all belong to the Tibeto-Chinese family and mainly to its Tibeto-Burman sub-family[17]." The dialects of this sub-family which are current in Assam belong in the main to three groups, viz. Naga spoken in the east of the Naga hills, *Kukichin spoken in Manipur, Cachar and the Lushai hills* and Bodo which claim practically all the surviving non-Aryan languages of the Brahmaputra valley, the Garo hills and North Cachar and it includes, among others, Kachari or Mech, Garo, Lalung, Rabha and Chutiya[18].

The theory of the entry of the Alpine and the Aryans into Assam seems to centre round the origin of the Kalitas who had an Alpine origin. The common belief is that the Kalitas or their ancestors entered India from the west, settled in Upper India, and ultimately entered Assam[19]. But when the Aryans entered Assam from the west is uncertain. It seems probably that the Aryan penetration into Assam began from the time of the Brahmanas and the Epics and by the 3rd century A.D. Aryan culture became the predominant culture in the

Brahmaputra valley due to the influence of the Hindu priests in whom the strain of the Aryan blood was very thin which was due largely to the absorbent power of Hinduism. On the Surma valley various communities now regarded as Hindu castes consist largely of aboriginal elements and the Koch of the Brahmaputra valley become a caste which admits proselytes from the ranks of the Kachari and other aboriginal tribes to Hinduism.[20] It may be safely assumed that philological changes were accompanied by racial fusion and the Aryans succeeded in imposing their language on the older inhabitants whose identity gradually became merged in that of their conquest.

Next, "early in the 13th century a hoard of hardy hillmen wandered into the eastern extremity of the Brahmaputra valley, led by chance rather than by any deep-seated design, and quite unconscious of the fact that their descendants were destined to bring the whole valley under their rule....[21] These were the progenitors of the Ahoms who were genuine Shans of southern Mongolian stock. A branch to which they belonged had long occupied the northern and eastern hill tracts of Upper Burma. Their physical type is unmistakably Mongoloid, and their language, script and ancient traditions are closely analogous to those of the great Shan race which spread eastwards from the border of Assam over nearly the whole of India, further and far into the interior of China. the Ahoms possessed the natural characteristics of a mountaineering people and were conspicuous for their great physical strength and hardihood, their heroism and love of independence. In course of their long residence in Assam, the Ahoms, though rising in the scale of civilization and gaining proficiency in the arts of peace, became gradually soft and luxuriant, and after a time abandoned their tribal dialect in favour of Assamese and identified themselves as Hindus. They had been assimilated into the Assamese society.[22]

The last element in pre-British Assamese society were the Muslims who were originally a Nordic people but had settled in the valleys. The geographical proximity of Kamrupa to Muslim Bengal led to several Muslim invasions of the Province. In course of these invasions thousands of Mahammadans settled in the valleys and Hajo became a stronghold of the Islamic culture and settlement.[23]

Social Structure

Pre-British Assamese society consisted of (i) the ruling aristocracy, (ii) subordinate officialdom, (iii) common subjects called "paiks", (iv) and the professional groups like (a) traders and merchants, (b) craftsmen, (c) free ryots or subjects. The ruling aristocracy consisted of the (i) high Ministers of the State called Patra Mantris, Bura Gohain, Bor Gohain, Bar Patra Gohain; (ii) Bar Phukans; (iii) Bar Baruahs. The lesser officers of the state called Phukans, Hazarikas, Barkatakis, Rajkhowas, together with Baruhas, Hati Baruahs, Bharalis, Saikias, Barbaruas and Baras constituted the middle stratum of Ahom society.[24] Besides, these Deodhains who constituted the priestly class in Ahom society occupied a prestigeous position since they were the custodians of knowledge of the Tai people.[25]

The Ahom community was divided into seven "phoids" or clans. Of these one provided the kings, a second provided the Bar Gohains, a third had the privilege to provide the Bura Gohains of the Ahom Government. The other clans provided other officers of the State. The clans were known after the place of their settlement. There were about 60 houses (families) which were just below the king in rank and were maintained by the State. After that some 57 families were exempt from taxes. Next to them there were 621 families which had the privilege of paying light revenue in cash. There was no caste system among the Ahoms.[26]

The entire adult population, however, was divided into "Khels" and all members of the "Khels" were termed as "Pyke". All members of the different "Khels" which varied from 1,000 to 5,000 were organized into "Gots" of four to three members each. One of the four or three members of each "Got" was in the service of the State by rotation. The "Pykes" enjoyed certain amount of revenue-free land holding and did not pay revenue for that. But each "Pyke" served for some time in his "Khel" and during his absence, the other members of the "Khel" looked after his holding.[27]

The pre-Ahom population of Assam known as the Brahmins, Kalitas, Koches, etc., were either appropriated within the "Khels" or remained outside it as free ryots and professionals who paid cash revenue to the state and the priestly class which continued to enjoy revenue free holdings. Of these people the Brahmins enjoyed more prestige and respect and held the highest position in society.[28] Caste system had continued to provide a structure to this society.[29] It is, of course, interesting to note that outsiders like Shabuddin Talash divided the people of Assam into two divisions, Kalitas and Assamese (Ahom).

A good Muslim population had grown in the valley of the Brahmaputra as a result of the Ahom-Mughal relations referred to before. The Muslims were regarded by the people of Asssam as outcasts and were put under social disabilities. It is held that later on seven noble families had settled around Sibsagar. One of these rose in prominence and held the position of general (Phukan) in the Ahom army.[30] During the reign of Rudra Singh (1699-1714) 18 more families came to settle in Assam. These were professional people who provided Persian scholars and writers, calligraphists or engravers, stone cutters, thread-cutters, miners, tailors and weavers.[31]

Slavery was at recognized institution of the Pre-British Assamese society.[32] Slaves were sold and purchased like merchandise. The king and his nobles owned slaves. They received slaves as presents, captured others in battles and frays and even purchased them from the market. The common people and priests also purchased slaves to work on their private estates or households. The price of a slave depended on his or her caste, the price of a high caste man being Rs. 20 and that of a low caste girl being Rs. 3. Hamilton writes that a Koch boy cost Rs. 25 and a Kolita Rs. 550. Girls were purchased mainly by the prostitutes.[33]

An important characteristic of the pre-British Assamese society was its catholicity. Though the Ahoms in the initial stages tried to maintain their separate identity and superiority by preserving the high offices of the State for themselves and exogamous marriages, gradually they threw open offices. to talented non-Ahoms and adopted endogamy. Subsequently the Ahoms adopted Hinduism as their religion and were thus absorbed within the socio-cultural environment of their conquered country. The Brahmins of Assamese society were less orthodox and this facilitated the adoption of tribal people to Hinduism.

Social distinctions

Pre-British Assamese society was feudalistic in structure.[34] There was a hierarchy of different grades of officers and classes of people and social distinctions and standards differed considerably. It was a special privilege of the king to live in a brick house having two round ends; nobles built houses with one round end and Deodhais had a similar privilege. None but the highest nobles had the right to wear shoes or travel in palanquins. Persons of humble birth who wished to wear wrappers or shawls were required to fold them over the left shoulder as the nobles were supposed to do over the right. Mahammadans, Morias and Doms and Haris were forbidden to wear their hair long and members of the latter classes were distinguished by tattoos of fish and broom on the foreheads.[35]

Organization

Assamese society was conditioned by the Hindu religion. A halo of divinity was created around the kingship. Family, the root of social structure, was patriarchal and joint family as usual unless the family had become large enough to break up into several smaller ones. Usually old parents and children of the parents lived under the same roof. Reverence to parents and older generation was inculcated through religion. Of course peculiar Ahom revenue system made the economic bondage of the family loose. Polygamy among the upper classes was common, general people were by and large monogamous. Polyandry was not recognized.[36] Pre-marital relation in Assam society is still permitted and lovers at mature age usually escape from their respective families during Bihu festival and after a period of absconding return to live as husband and wife.

Position of women

"Women in Assam enjoyed more freedom than their sisters in other parts of India; their movements were free and many acquired learning.[37] Women were refined and enlightened and active and versatile in their accomplishments." Suklenmung, popularly known as

Gargaiya Raja, added a new minister called Barpatra Gohain under the influence of his Queen Chan-ching. Gaurinath Singha consulted his mother on affairs of State. Ligiris, as the dancing girls were known, were attached to temples, households of the princes and nobles. One such ligiri was married to the Ahom King Siba Singha (A.D. 1714-1744) and became the chief queen.[38] Widow remarriage was discouraged and yet some princesses were remarried several times with no social stigma. Some ahom women were gallant and Mula-Gabharu did actual fighting in the battlefield. The legendary Joymati gallantly faced inhuman suffering for political reasons[39]

Towards the close of the Ahom regime, however society sunk to the lowest rung of degeneration. Maniram Dewan observed that during the calamitous days of 1794 Burkendazes introduced the habit of eating opium, bhang; and during the rule of the Burmese opium-eating became a popular vice. People became lazy and indolent, they took to sale of wives and children.[40] **Alamgirnama** of Mohammed Cazim speaks of the Assamese society in the following terms: "They are a base and unprincipled nation, and have no fixed religion. They follow no rule, but that of their own inclination; and make the approbation of their own vicious minds the best of the propriety of their action. Their strength and courage are apparent in their looks, but their ferocious manners, and brutal tempers, are also betrayed by their physiognomy. They are superior to most nations in corporal force, and hardy exertions. They are enterprising, savage, fond of war, vindictive, treacherous, and deceitful. The virtues of compassion kindness, friendship, sincerity, truth, honour, good faith, shame, and purity of morals have been left out of their composition. The seeds of tenderness and humanity have not been sown in the field of their frames.[41]

Robinson's observation in the early years of British rule supports the above view. He writes: "Morality is in its lowest ebb. If the vices of lying, deceit, dishonesty and impurity in all its forms, can degrade a people, then the Assamese have sunk to the utmost depth of human depravity.... In no respect are the native manners more deficient, than in filial and conjugal fidelity. The women, to say the least, are notoriously corrupt, and totally devoid of delicacy, their language is often gross and disgusting. Their terms of abuse and reproach are indelicate to the utmost degree.[42]

Economy and Occupations

Pre-British Assamese people were by and large a rural people who lived in small villages consisting of several huts. Houses built of brick and mortar were forbidden for the common man.[43] There were some towns which had a little higher population and which had come into existence around the administrative centres like Rangpur, Gargaon, Tezpur and Gauhati. Of the few towns of the Ahom kingdom Gauhati and Goalpara had begun to develop modern urban character when large business organizations and trade posts began to grow during the closing years of the Ahom kingdom as a result of rise of trade and commerce.[44]

Ahom economy was preponderantly rural-agricultural. People lived on agriculture and sericulture and very few depended on any trade and commerce. Some sort of trade with the neighbouring hills existed; a few people traded with Bengal. Industry worth the term, except small-scale weaving in every household, did not exist. Production was on local consumption level. A limited number of smiths, ivory and metal works kept alive industrial activities. Almost every household produced all that it required and there were no such people as barbers, carpenters, washermen or fishermen.[45]

Social mobility was practically non-existent. The governing aristocracy was hereditary to begin with and administrative jobs were confined to some families of the Ahoms and jobs passed down to sons according to the law of primogeniture, unless the son was otherwise incapacitated. There was extremely limited scope for the common people to rise to the rank of aristocracy and high office, though socially there was no bar for the common people to rise to higher positions.[46]

Standard of Living

In spite of social distinctions, life of the people was plentiful and easy. The fertility of the soil gave an average Assamese more than enough leisure as little toil produced abundant necessaries. In lower Assam people used silver ornaments and cotton cloth but in Upper Assam as plenty of gold was available people used gold ornaments and conditions being favourable people there produced enough silk and wore silken linen.[47]

Recreation and Past-times

Life of the people of Assam in pre-British days was not drab and without any diversions. At the accession of every king a series of ceremonies and sports were arranged for over a week. These included spectacular fight of elephants, buffaloes, and tigers. Royal tours and hunting expeditions provided change in daily life.[48] Ahom kings were very fond of aviaries and maintained officers to train birds for sport. The trainers of victorious birds were rewarded and those of defeated ones were punished. Besides religious festivities, like Durga Puja, Holi, etc., Bihus and theatrical performances (Bhaonas) provided relief to the multitudes.[49]

Learning and Literature

The concept of State responsibility to provide mass education is a new thing. Yet, as in other parts of India so also in the Ahom kingdom, the kings patronized educational institutions and grants were liberally assigned to learned scholars. The Head Pandit of the kingdom was given 20 attendants and a grant of 100 puras of land. Those who aspired for education went to either Tols or Satras where Sanskrit education was imparted.[50] The Ahom priests, that is the Deodhains or Bailungs, inculcated Tai education and trained the high officers of the State in Buranjis or history of the Ahoms and procedure of social and religious ceremonies.[51] Many students were sent to Nabadurip in Bengal for Sanskrit learning.[52] Crafts and arts were learnt by apprenticeship from the master craftsmen and artists. Modes of warfare and strategies of fighting were taught as and when necessary to those engaged in the forces of the kingdom.[53]

Pre-British Assamese literature flourished considerably as a result of royal patronage and encouragement by wealthy nobles. There took place a healthy growth of both literature and music. To begin with the writers of the age were engaged in Assamese rendering of the Sanskrit texts like the Puranas and the Epics, Hitapadesha and Panchatantra and composed panegyrics and ballads for their patrons.[54] Writing of Buranjis which was an Ahom practice in Tai language, in course of time, was introduced in Assamese literature as well. With the passage of time secular literature and works on erotics and surology, medicine for both human beings and domestic animals and astrology and art began to appear. The greatest contribution to Assamese literature of the age is the art of writing Buranjis or historical books which provide a fairly reliable account of the Ahom period and the Vamsabalis *which are biographical accounts of the noble families*. The literary works of the Vaishnava saints, Sankaradeva and Madhavadeva, shed lusture on the Assamese life and literature even today and are yet to be surpassed in grandeur and style.

Religion and popular beliefs

By far the most popular religion in Assam before the annexation by the British was Hinduism in different forms, e.g. Saivism, Vaishnavism, Tantricism.[55] The architectural remains throughout the length and breadth of the country bear clear testimony as do the profuse Sanskrit literature of the age. The remains of Tezpur, Malinithan, Bhismaknagar show that Vishnu, Lakshmi, Siva and Parbati were worshipped and beautiful decorative temples were dedicated to them. After the Ahom kings became Hindu converts a series of temples for Siva and Durga were constructed under royal patronage and arrangements for regular worship in them were made by assignment of "paiks" and lands. The worship of goddess Durga during autumn, the celebration of Doljatra (Holi), and observance of Siva Ratri were arranged at the capital town.[56] The age-old temple of Kamakhya at Gauhati and Silghat continued to receive as much reverence as was shown to the new dieties in the capital. And the Ahoms continued to patronize, even after their conversion to Hinduism, their ancestral tribal gods and goddesses who were worshipped by the Deodhais, in the traditional manner.

But in spite of the virility of Saivism, Tantricism, devotional Vaishnavism captured the imagination of the masses. In mediaeval India a wave of devotionalism spread far and wide and Assam caught the contagion in the 15th century. The old Brahmanical faith had degenerated in Assam, situated as it was in an isolated position sorrounded by hills and covered by forests, and lack of contact with the main founts of Brahamanism in India resulted in accommodation in religious tastes and practices of all sorts of corruption and superstition. In such a situation Sri Sankaradeva (A.D. 1449-1568,) appeared as a socio-religious reformer

The simple folk of Assam were easily captivated by elaborate and magnificent ceremonies performed to worship the majestic images of the Hindu pantheon and when the ingenious priests could connect them with such deities naturally they felt elated and became conscious followers of their mythological progenitors; little did they understand the ceremonial practices accompanying their worship of different deities. But the degeneration must have caught the attention of the intelligensia and the natural outcome was devotionalism of Vaishnava religion which declared in clear terms that the only way to God lay in invocation of god or recitation of His praise with pure devotion in vernacular. Sankaradeva, the propagator of the new faith, would not allow even to associate the name of Radha who represented a true female devotee of Lord Krishna in his system of devotion to Vishnu-Krishna. Later on his disciple Madhavadeva, of course, could allow a little catholicity and Radha-Krishna cult now gained a little popularity.[57]

Besides the Brahmanical Hinduism and devotionalism of the Neo-Vaishnavism, there were a few Buddhists in Upper Assam and the followers of Islam. The Buddhist and immigrated from south-west China and were followers of the Mahajana sect and followers of the Prophet belonged to the Sunni branch of Islam. The bulk of the tribal people, of course, followed their ancestral tribal religion.[58]

Assam, a stronghold of Tantricism at one time, continued to believe in the efficacy of sacrifices and divination. Astrologers found favour with the kings, nobles and common people alike. The use of charms and incantations for winning battles and destruction of enemies was a commo practice. The Ahom soldiers are said to have prayed to goddess Kamakshyaya before the battle of Saraighat: "O Mother Kamakshya, eat up the Mughals and give us victory." Dr. Wade writes about superstition: "Recent fortification of the mountain sunk three feet, the barrels stalk afforded no grain and a scarcity prevailed in the kingdom, thousands and thousands of sparrows, hawks were observed to abandon the western provinces and float in the air of Upper Assam, while the bamboos which surrounded the habitations of man exhibited flowers in bloom."[59]

Art, Architecture and Painting

The Ahoms who ruled almost for six hundred years were great patrons of art, architecture and painting. The palaces of the monarchs at the capital towns Gargaon and Rangpur, the very many temples all over the kingdom from Kamakhya in Gauhati to Siva temple in Sibsagar, and the sculptures inside the royal houses and temples and the design of the bridges, palaces and temples even today bear testimony to the refinement in these spheres of human activity. Though the buildings and temples of the Ahom kings were not gigantic and greater in magnitude as were the Mughal mousalems and forts, yet their architectural design, layout and exquisite finish betray wonderful developments in these spheres.[60]

Painters themes were primarily religious and natural objects and many beautiful scenes based on the Bhagabata and Puranas were meticulously depicted by the artists of the period. Besides the religious paintings a good many painters drew pictures of wild animals and other beasts of sport.[61]

Race relation in Pre-British Days

Shutup in the valley of the Brahmaputra by hills and forests, through 600 years of Ahom rule, nay Assam through ages down to the British annexation, the Assamese forged a catholic social structure out of their heterogeneous ethnic and linguistic groups and united the different ethnic and linguistic people on the basis of Hindu culture and Aryan language. Yet Assam never remained totally isolated from the mainstream of Indian culture. Her art and architecture, literature and language, crafts and cargoes, religions and superstitions-all bear ample testimony to the fact that Assam drew her inspiration and cultural sustenance from outside Assam without any prejudice and on the basis of original Kirat foundation built a beautiful edifice which is the Assamese culture of today.

A conspicuous feature of Assamese history to the close of the Ahom rule is the absence of separative ethnic consciousness or racial feeling and consequent social disturabance or political riots. Throughout the length of history of Assam, we find Assam was regarded as an integral part of Bharatbarsa and people from beyond the bounds of Assam were wellcomed to enrich her culture and civilization. Many of them who settled in Assam made significant contributions to the Assamese culture. Even the Muslims who had invaded the country were not exterminated as enemies and allowed to take up employment with the Ahom Government and accorded social status.

The only evidence of social disturbance was the outbreak of Moamaria rebellion. The Moamarias are a sect of Vaisnavas who followed one God Krishna-Vishnu as enunciated by Srimanta Sankaradeva. The followers were known by an epithet Moamaria because most of them lived on fishing a kind of fish called locally as "Moa"; those who caught this kind of fish were known as Moamaria. Though Vaishnava by faith, these people were not vegetarian and chiefly the converts were aboriginals of Upper Assam and belonged to the Cachari group of people. In the 17th and 18 the centuries they had become highly organized under "Satras" which were looked after by religious preachers styled Mahantas.

Meanwhile the Ahom princes had begun to be charmed by Brahmanism. When a link with the founder king of the Ahom dynasty with a Hindu God-King was established and the Brahmin priests extended material help to the princes, the Ahom kings began to patronize Brahmanical religion. The spread of Vaishnava faith threatened the existence of the priestly class, the vanguard of Sakta religion, the former began to put all sorts of obstacles on Vaishnava followers and even humiliated their spiritual heads. This made the new proselytes discontented and when the Ahom monarchy towards the closing period tended to become autocratic and oppressive, the Vaishnavas rebelled against the Ahom authority.[62] The Ahom king was driven out and the rebel leaders assumed royal pretentions. But their incapacity and excesses again brought in counter-rebellion and the Ahom monarchy was restored.

NOTES

1. E. Gait, *A History of Assam* pp. 10-23
2. M. L. Bose, *Development of administration in Assam.*
3. Ibid.

4. Ibid.
5. Ibid.
6. *Assam Administration Report, 1874-76.*
7. Ibid.
8. Ibid.
9. A Amanatulla, *A History of Cooch Behar.*
10. S.N. Bhattacharya, *A History of the Mughal North-East Frontier* J.N. Sarkar, *Life of Mirjumla.*
11. S.K. Bhuya, *Anglo-Asamese Relations,* p. 270-71.
12. *Assam Administration Report, 1874-76.*
13. Ibid.
14. A.C. Banarjee, Eastern Frontier of British India.
15. Ibid.
16. G. Grjerson, *Linguistic Survey of India* Vol. II. p. 561-621.
17. Ibid.
18. Ibid.
19. B. Kakati, Kalita Jatir Ibbritiya (History of the Kalitas)
20. ibid.
21. *Assam Administration Report 1874-76*, Part II.
22. Ibid.
23. *An Account of Assam and its Administration.*
24. B. Shirma (ed), Dr. Wade's *Account of Assam,* pp. VI-XXXVIII.
25. S.R. Bhuyan (ed), *An Account of Assam* by C. Hamilton, pp. 4-5.
26. Ibid.
27. Ibid.
28. S.K. Bhuyan (ed.), *an Account of Assam,* pp. 51-57.
29. Ibid.
30. H.K. Barpuzan, *Assam in the days of the Company*, p. 264.
31. Ibid.
32. "Slavery in Assam," Dr. (Mrs) S.L. Baruah, *Journal of Historical Research*, Dibrugarh University, Vol. II, 1977; Gait *A History of Assam*,X
33. Ibid. Hamilton, *An Account of Assam.*
34. Gait, *A History of Assam*, X. Hamilton - *An Account of Assam*, p. 16.
35. H.D. Phukan - *Assam Buranji* p. 89.
36. N.K. Basu, *Assam in the Ahom Age*, pp. 255-281.
37. Ibid.
38. Ibid.
39. Ibid.
40. Memorial submitted to A.J.M. Mill in 1853, Prof. Mohendra Bara in his *Assam in 1857* quotes Maniram Dewan to support the above statement and Prof. Bara holds that the Dewan made "and honest assessment" of the condition of the country (see *Assam in 1857* by Mahendra Bara, Gauhati, 1957, pp. 17-18; p- 19). Prof. M. Neog in his *Pracasasanavali* includes an inscription on sale of wife - p. 72.

    If may be observed here "that Cooch-Behar which because a separate State and stood between Bengal and Assam had almost similar practices. In 1783 Turner leading British Embassy Tibet wrotes: "If a Reiat, or a peasant, owes a sum of money, and has not the ability to satisfy his creditor, he is compelled to give up his wife as a pledge, and possession of her is kept until the debt is discharged. It sometimes 'happens,' as they affirm. that the wife of a debtor is not redemed for the space of one, two, or three years; and then if, during her residence and connection with the creditor, a family should have been the consequence, half of it is considered as the property of the person with whom she lived and half that of the real husband." Regarding the sale of children Turner wrote: "The lower rank without scruple dispose of their children for slaves, to any purchaser, and that too for a very trifling consideration; nor yet, though in a traffic so unnatural, is the agency of a third person ever employed. Nothing is more common than to see a mother dress up her child, and bring it to market, with no other hope, no other view, than to enhance the price she may procure for it." Capt. Samual Turner, *Bhutan and Tibet, An Account of an Embassy to the court of the Teshoo Lama in Tibet*, pp. 10-11.

41. Md. Cazim, a writer of the 17th century, was quoted by Robinson to support his observation in the first half of the 19th century. See Robinson's *A Descriptive Account of Assam* pp. 255.
42. Ibid., (It is necessary to verify foreign writer's account by contemporary indegenous accounts for a foreigner thinks everything in an alien country absurd and inferior for the things are not in his own ways of acting and thinking and cannot be cut out by his own measures or suited to his own standards.)
43. Hamilton, op. cit.
44. Ibid.
45. Pembston.
46. Wade, Op. cit.
47. Pembston; op.cit.
48. Hamilton, op. cit.
49. Ibid.
50. Ibid.
51. N.K. Basu, op. cit. pp. 238-81
52. Ibid.
53. Ibid.
54. M. Neog, *A New Light on the History of Asamiya Literature*.
55. "Culture of the North-East Frontier" M.L. Bose, published in SHODHAK, Vol. V. 1975.
56. Ibid.
57. N.K. Basu, op. cit., pp. 223-250.
58. Wade, op. cit. See *Tepography of Assam*.
59. Ibid.
60. S. Borkotoki, *Assam-Land and People*.
61. N.K. Basu, op. Cit., pp. 312-319.
62. N.K. Basu, op. Cit., pp. 223-250.

FIVE

Demography of Assam

Assam at the close of the Ahom rule had become a thinly populated province. From the middle of the 18th century secetarian wars had caused much bloodshed and civil strife and ultimately this invited Burmese interference in Assam. The Burmese interference again brought in its trail devastating wars in course of which thousands were massacred and villages after villages were destroyed. Many thousands ran away in panic into the dense forests of Cachar hills to find way to the Surma Valley and others moved towards the lower valley of the Brahmaputra; when the Burmese retreated to Burma, they carried away with them not less than 30,000 as captives or slaves; no lesser a number was captured as slaves by the Singphos who crept down the Patkai after the Burmese had laid waste upper Assam.[1] Therefore when the British came to occupy Assam, there were not enough people to give them even the necessary supply of foodstuff and porters required for the garrisons and reconstruction of channels of communication. As such when the new industries were started and transportation channels began to be constructed, labourers had to be imported into the province from different parts of India.

During the British rule of 122 years (1826-1947) the political map of Assam underwent revolutionary changes. Assam in 1826, that is, at the cessation of the first Anglo-Burmese war, meant more or less the Brahmaputra valley, excluding the district of Goalpara and Eastern Duars. The total area was estimated in 1840 to be 3,500 sq. miles including Goalpara and Eastern Duars and the population was supposed to be 700,000 including the Bengalis of Goalpara.[2] These figures were multiplied as a result of (i) addition of territories to Assam; (ii) influx of tenants or peasants to settle on fallow lands; (iii) importation of labour from different parts of India; (iv) employment of "outsiders" in Assam Administration; (v) voluntary settlement of professional groups; (vi) immigration of traders and businessmen from other parts of the country.

Perusal of the political history of Assam between 1826 and 1947 shows that the contiguous territories of Assam, viz. the hills on both sides of the river Brahmaputra and the attachment of the valleys of the Barak and Surma, the Dewani districts of Sylhet and Goalpara and Eastern Duars expanded the territories of Assam considerably. In 1874-76 the total area of Assam was 55, 384 sq. miles.[3] In 1874-76 the territories annexed to Assam Administration were calculated at 14,447 sq. miles of hills between the two valleys of the Brahmaputra and the Barak and Surma, 6,668 sq. miles of plains territories of the districts of Sylhet and Cachar, besides the district of Goalpara sq. 4,334 miles) and Eastern Duars (15,68 sq. miles).[4] This calculation leaves out the entire territory of the North-East Frontier, that is, the modern provinces of Arunachal Pradesh (32,000 miles) and Mizoram (8,142 sq. miles), not to speak of Manipur (8,620 sq. miles in 1941). Thus in 1901 the valley of the Brahmaputra occupied a part only of the total area of the provinces 56,243 sq. miles of a total of 67,834 sq. miles.[5] Thus Assam proper which formed the Ahom State before the formation of the British province of Assam lost its physical form.

Along with the change of the political map, the demographic map of Assam underwent a radical change as well. In 1835 the population of Assam valley districts including Goalpara (100,000) was estimated at 700,000,[6] in 1874-76; it rose to 4,132,019.[7] In 1901 the population of five Brahmaputra valley districts rose to 2.62 millions; the population of the province of Assam as a whole rose to 6,126,945.[8] In 1941, of the total of 10,930,388 population of Assam valley accounted for 2,804,202 only.[9]

The first and foremost cause of rise in the population of the province of Assam of the British Empire was annexation of contiguous territories. The first territory annexed to Assam was the district of Goalpara (4,433 sq.miles) and Eastern Duars (1,568 sq. miles). Goalpara and Eastern Duars formed originally a part of the Dewani Suba of Bengal. Its population of 444, 761 souls (1870) of Goalpara were mostly Bengalis and the people of Eastern Duars who numbered 37,047 in 1870 were tribal people who could be assimilated with either Assamese or Bengali people following a liberal policy of acculturation.[10] The population of Goalpara district with which was tagged Eastern Duars rose to 46,200 in 1901;[11] in 1947 the population rose to 1,014,285.[12]

The next territory (6,157 sq. miles) added were the tribal hills of the Khasis and Jaintias. The United Khasi and Jaintia hills were inhabited by Austric Jaintia-Khasi tribes who had a matriarchal social organization. Neither in their language nor in their culture did these people have any similarity with the Assamese to whose province fate brought them for administrative purposes. The Khasi-Jaintias numbered 141,838 in 1874-76.[13] In 1901 the population of the Khasi-Jaintia hills rose to 202,250; in 1941 the total reached 332,251.[14] But as a result of transfer of the capital of Assam to Shillong in the Khasi hills, some Bengalis and negligible Assamese and a trading population immigrated to these hills.

We have already noticed the fact that in upper Assam an Ahom principality was restored in 1833 and the same was annexed to the Assam Administration in 1838. The territory of the principality was divided into two districts of Sibsagar and Lakhimpur. This addition of territory had increased the population of the Administration but since these people were of the same linguistic group and were in the process of assimilation with the Assamese society no socio-cultural problem arose out of this accession of territory. The same was the case with the two further small tracts of the Mattaks and Khamptis. When Mattak was attached to the British Administration the people brought under the Administration were of the same socio-linguistic-cultural group as were the Assamese and hence no problem from linguistic and cultural points of view cropped up. The dispossession of the Khampti chief from the south bank of the Lohit (Brahmaputra) river and consequent attachment of the tract to the Assam Administration added only Assamese people to the Lakhimpur district, created already by the bifurcation of the Ahom principality. The net result of these three annexations was an increase of population but these did not let loose any centrifugal tendency in these people.[15]

The creation of the Garo hills district and its accession to the Assam Administration resulted in an increase of yet another heterogeneous population of the province of Assam. The Garos, a kindred tribe of the Khasi-Jaintia hills, had also a matriarchal society and numbered, in 1872, 100,000 souls who lived over 3, 180 sq. miles of territory.[16] In 1901 their number increased to 138,274 and in 1941 they reached 223,569.[17] But the Garos remained a district and separate people within the province of Assam.

Similarly the constitution of the Naga hills district consisting of the Nagas of different tribes covering an area of 68,918 sq. miles and a population of 68,918 souls tagged to the Assam Administration, yet another heterogeneous element in the province.[18] The Nagas were a different people who had nothing in common with either the Assamese or the Garo, Khasi and Jaintia people who had been brought under the Assam Administration. These people gradually increased to 2671 in 1901[19] and in 1941 this a number swelled to 189,641.[20]

The transfer of Sylhet and Cachar in 1874 to the Assam Administration increased the territorial jurisdiction of the province by 5,440 and 3,750 sq. miles respectively. The populations of the two districts, 1,719,539 and 205,027, respectively were constituted of almost Bengalis with an insignificant intermixture of tribal Manipuris and tea garden labourers.[21] These two districts were separated from the other Bengali-speaking district of Goalpara by incommunicable hills of the Garos and Khasis. Separation from the people of Assam by hills and the contiguous province of Bengal from which the people drew their cultural sustenance kept these people a distinct Bengali community till the end of the British rule. The numerical strength rose to 1,370,024 in 1941.[22]

Further, constitution of the North Cachar and Mikir hills district and the Lushai hills district brought under the Assam Administration two further heterogeneous socio-linguistic areas. The area covered by these two districts was 5,883 miles and 8,142 (Lushai) sq. miles and their population numbered 14,321 and 63,430 respectively in 1901.[23] The population of Lushai hills rose to 152,786 in 1941.[24]

These two tribes were different in speech and socio-cultural habits from the rest of the population of the province of Assam.

Besides the annexation of the above districts the foot-hills areas of the present Arunachal Pradesh were added to the contiguous plains districts of the valley of the Brahmaputra. The increase of the territory did not result in an increase in the heterogeneous population under the Assam Administration as these territories were inhabited mostly by Assamese people. But the North-East Frontier hills, constituted into frontier Tracts in 1919, put under the Assam Administration a host of tribes and sub-tribes numbering 110 who were different from each other and had no similarity with the people of the Assam, living over 32,000 sq. miles of land.[25]

The growth and development of the tea industry in Assam during the British regime is the most significant part of the history of Assam and the other developments are either subsidiary or consequential practically as everything else was either contributory or resultant of the growth of tea industry. The second largest factor that contributed to the growth of population in Assam was the development of tea industry. The number of gardens had risen greatly than in 1905, to 998 in 1947, and 40,9000 persons were employed in the tea plantation in 1903 and by 1938 the number of persons employed in these rose to 531,000 persons.[26]

The tea gardens of Assam had begun to recruit labour from outside the province through contractors. These people went to tribal areas of central India and put before them false hopes to immigrate to Assam and take up employment in the tea gardens. These contractors were called "Coolie" catchers. In many cases young people, brothers, sons and even wives left their homes for a delightful future. The contractors' job was to transport the recruits to Assam and receive payment from the management counting heads without any regard to the capacity or willingness of the person concerned to serve. Therefore the management gradually took to the system of recruitment through the "Sardar" who was an old garden labourer. In such cases an old garden employee was given assistance to proceed to his native place and bring back with him a number of new recruits and for this the "Sardar" or the old garden employee was given a nice commission. To ward off the evil of breaking the tribal families, the system of transporting the entire family from original home to Assam began to be adopted. But though the "Sardari" system thus began to replace the old contractor" system, the contractors continued to transport tribal people from central India and dispose them of to the garden authorities at Dhubri, the gateway to Assam.

The tribal belt of the Chotta Nagpur area of Central provinces and Madras Presidency drew the imagination of the planters. Contractors were engaged to enlist and deport tribal people from these areas. Slave system had been abolished legally and yet it was that which was necessary for the successful operation of European tea plantation in Assam. So under the authority of law contractors went to unsophisticated tribal villages and put before them a romantic picture of free employment in a paradise under the patronage of the English. The destitute and hapless tribal people fell in the trap of the contractors who paid them some money in advance and even provided them journey expenses. Floods of immigrants began to enter Assam with new hopes and aspiration to be subjected to the inhuman bondage of slavery. The Bengal Administration Report for the year 1867-68 shows that of a total of 34,433 labourers in Assam plantations only 11,633 or one third only were local recruits and in 1872 the imported labour force stood at 24,000 in Assam proper and 20,000 in Cachar in spite of heavy death and desertation that occurred due to unhealthy living and working conditions. Yet in 1901 one-twelfth of the total population of Assam was this labour. The total population of this labour force swelled to 417,262 in 1905,[27] and in 1947 it reached 954000.[28] There was practically not a single labourer in 1947 who was originally an inhabitant of Assam.

The plantation labour was multilingual and heterogenous. In 1884-85, 44.7 per cent were from Chotanagpur, 27.2 per cent from Bengal, 21.6 per cent from U. P. and Bihar, 0.2 per cent from Bombay Presidency and 0.7 per cent from Madras Presidency; only 55 per cent were local recruits.[29] In 1901, 148,500 persons were brought from United Provinces, Bengal and Bihar, 177,100 from Santal Parganas and Chotanagpur area, 55,600 from Central provinces, 12,500 from Madras Presidency and only some 10,200 were recruited locally from amongst the ex-garden labour stock.[30] In 1930 the United Provinces, Bengal and Bihar provided some 216,500 labour to Assam Tea Gardens, 193,600 came from Saube parganas and Chotanagpur area, 78,200 were supplied by the Central Provinces. Madras sent 59500 and 9200 came from other places. The local recruits provided 65,100 hands.[31]

The Tea District Labour Association compiled a book on castes and tribes of the plantation labour. It shows that all the people of the labour force were, without exception, people of the tribal stock of Kolarian or Austric or Dravidian origin. They spoke different dialects rather than languages and had different socio-religious customs and manners. In the new home excluded from free communication with the Assamese or adjacent tribal communities of Assam, these people developed a new form of speech to communicate with each other and the management. This new speech known as garden labour language was a mixed language developed by a mixture of Hindustani, Bengali and Assamese vocabulary. In course of generations many of the tea garden labourers left their jobs in the garden and took up cultivation and settled in the valley.[32]

Besides the plantation industry, there were two other industries which imported non-Assamese population in Assam. They were coal and petroleum industries in Lakhimpur district. Petroleum discovered right after the annexation (1825) was drilled only after 1866 and Assam Oil Company which acquired the right to produce oil transferred its management to Burmah-Shell in 1920. The industry produced crude oil and refined it at a refinery built at Digboi. Labour requirement was inconsequential but the technical and clerical jobs were monopolized by the Bengali immigrants or people of Surma valley; the upper posts, of course, remained a preserve of the white people. The total employment came to 8,832 in 1931.[33]

The coal-mining industry in Upper Assam as undertaken by the Assam Railway Trading Company which operated railway line between Dibrugarh and Sadiya from 1882. Coal was necessary to run the railway. Steamships and tea gardens required coal for their factories. Therefore this Company began to mine coal from the Margherita-Ledo area. Coal-mines in Upper Assam were discovered as early as 1825 but production was undertaken only after the completion of railways in Upper Assam and development of plantation industries. As the tea industry faced the problem of labour, so also the coal industry, the labour, mainly Nepali, who were thrown out of employment after the completion of railway lines, was absorbed in coal industry. But the nature of employment did not attract the Nepali immigrants to go for such employment. Therefore recourse was taken to importation of tribal people from Telegu territories of the south and in course of time mining became practically dependent on Telengi labour. The number employed by all the coal-mines of Assam rose to 7,325 in 1941.[34] The head office of Coal and Railways operated from Margherita and office employment was monopolized by the Bengalis. Here also the superior posts were kept aside for the white people. The coal mines in the Jeypur area were, of course, not operated by the A. R. T. Company; it was explored by Rajasthani traders who did not employ much imported labour as did the A. R. T. Company.

The other coal-mines in the then Assam at Cherrapunjee area did not import labour from outside. Coal-mining in the hills was not undertaken seriously, as production and transportation both were expensive and local demand for coal was not enough to call for increased production. However as mines in this region did not add to immigration figures the operation of this industry does not interest us; this did not bring about any significant change in the society of the province as well.

Assam during the British period did not have any large-scale industry other than these. There was only a small match factory at Dhubri in Goalpara district operated by a Swedish Company since 1815.

The third important contributing factor to the growth of population of Assam was the immigration of the Muslim peasants or cultivators from adjacent East Bengal districts of the Bengal Presidency. Though in Assam a lot of fallow and waste land was available after the British annexation people were not available to come and settle on land. In 1891 the Census Commission reported that in spite of plentiful land immigration of peasants was insignificant.[35] There were some marginal cases of immigration in the last two decades of the 19th century. But the nature and effect of the immigration is best expressed in the language of the Census Commissioner of 1891: "Indian peasants are ignorant and wanting in energy and enterprise and slow to leave their homes. Coolies of the gardens come to Assam because they are more than usually indigent and are especially recruited and brought to the province at the expense of persons for whom they are to labour. No such inducement exists to bring ryot to Assam to take up land for cultivation and they therefore do not come. A certain number of persons from the neighbouring Bengal districts of Mymensing, Dacca and Rangpur have crossed the boundary and settled down in Sylhet and Goalpara but this can scarcely be called immigration. They have only moved a few miles from their original homes and accident of boundary alone has brought them within the limits of Assam. Practically the only real and permanent immigrants are the Coolies, who come up under labour contracts and settle down in the province after their agreements have expired."[36]

But the nature of agricultural immigration changed in the very next decade. The partition of Bengal and the creation of Eastern Bengal and Assam province for the first time caught the imagination of the Muslim leaders of the rising anti-Congress Muslim League party who dreamt of colonizing Assam and lay a claim to Assam for inclusion in Pakistan, should the partition demand come true. Waves of immigrants began to sweep over the bordering Assam districts of Goalpara and Kamrup and in the following decade they penetrated through Darrang and Nowgong districts of central Assam to Sibsagar and the Lakhimpur districts. The Government sympathy for the Muslim leadership between 1921 and 1942 as a result of noncooperation of the Congress helped the immigration process to flourish at a steady rate.

A HORDE OF LAND-HUNGRY IMMIGRANTS

The Census Commissioner of 1931 wrote, "probably the most important event in the province during the last twentyfive years, an event moreover which seems likely to alter permanently the whole future of Assam and to destroy more surely than did the Burmese invasion of 1820 the whole structure of Assamese culture and civilization, has been the invasion of a vast horde of land-hungry Bengali immigrants-mostly Muslims from the districts of East Bengal and in particular from Mymensing. The first army corps which followed them in the years 1921-31 has consolidated their position in that district and has also completed the conquest of Nowgong. The

Barapeta subdivision of Kamrup has also fallen to their attack and Darrang is being invaded."[37]

The growth of Muslim immigration to Assam was facilitated by several other factors as well. The development of communication, particularly railways and regular steamer services between Assam and Bengal through the river Barak or Surma and Brahmaputra facilitated the movement of people from Eastern Bengal. And when the Muslim leaders spoke to the East Bengal people of the availability of land, cheap cost of living, the poor people in quest of land came out of their ancestral home. In 1883 under government subsidy a daily steamer service was introduced between Assam and Bengal through the river Brahmaputra and in 1887 a similar service was introduced through the Surma river under improved conditions; it now took seven days to reach Dibrugarh from Goalundo which previously required three weeks or more time. On the Railway side the Assam Bengal Railways was opened to traffic from Chittagong to Lumding through Tripura, Sylhet, Cachar and North Cachar Hills. Then Lumding was connected to Gauhati and Dibrugarh. The construction of railway lines in Kamrup and Goalpara thus connecting Bengal with Assam further facilitated the movement of people from East Bengal to Assam.

The allied profession of agriculture, animal husbandry, also contributed not insignificant to the growth of population in Assam during the British regime. Animal husbandry as a district profession did not exist in pre-British Assam. Though milk was not an unpopular item of diet of the non-tribal Assam population no professional milkman supplied this commodity to the society and stock raising for consumption was yet to be known.

Animal husbandry and stock raising had became a monopoly of Nepali people. After Assam had became a part of the British territory, people from Nepal began to migrate to the neighbouring province of Assam to engage themselves in employment. To begin with these people were required as porters and labourers. In 1931, 3,000 were found in Naga hills, 2.000 in Mizo hills and 3,000 were engaged in Manipur; but by far the largest number were found in Khasi-Jaintia hills.[38] In the hill areas they served as porters or labourers but some were, especially in Shillong, engaged in grazing, and many found employment in the army deployed in North-East Frontier. With the growth of urban centres and new professional classes dependent on service therein, demand for milk was created and now these Nepali people took to cattle rearing for production of milk in the vast fallow lands of the hills and plains of Assam.

The immigration of Nepali graziers as a phenomenon of growth of population became distinct from the beginning of the present century. Quite a good number was found settled over Kamrup (8527 in 1921), Darrang (1,899 in 1921) and Khasi-Jaintia hills in the first two decades of the present century but in the 1930 they spread over the adjoining Nowgong and Darrang (40,000 in 1931) districts and few approached Lakhimpur (11,951 in 1931) district on the north bank. The Nepali population which accounted for 20,193 in the 1901 census rose to 47,654 in 1911; in 1921 their number grew to 70,344 but highest growth was noticed during 1921-31, the figure of 88,306 being reached in 1931.[39]

The cause of Nepali immigration in such large numbers has not been studied in depth. After the Anglo-Nepalese war of 1814-16 in the middle of the last century the Anglo-Nepali relations began to improve and after the Sepoy Mutiny a large number of them were employed in the British Indian Army. The Gorkha Regiment played a significant role in the British conquest of Indian territories; they were deployed even in Burma and Malay Peninsula. But what led to immigration to Assam is uncertain. "The barren rocky ranges of hills and narrow unhealthy valleys around the capital Kathmundu were unsuited for lucrative cultivation; with an increase in population there living became difficult.[40] The ambition of Nepal to push forward to west had been frustated with limits fixed at the Sutlej. On the western frontier while they had been checkmated by the Sikhs, the Southern border was completely sealed against them by the British throughout from the west to east. As Nepal had come to feel stabilizing its occupation with boundary at Tista in the east there was no question of expanding the line on this side. Nepal thus was confined to a defined stretch of territories about this time with no opportunity to expand on either side."[41] It is probable that the British after the Mutiny accorded the Napalis free movement in India and after Assam was annexed to British Empire large numbers of them were recruited for serving as porters and labourers in the new province. After the mid-century Tibetan expedition a large number of the soldiers were demobilized. Easy life in Assam by cultivation and cattle rearing definitely attracted them but the reason why tradition-bound people ventured to such distant country for livelihood is a curious phenomenon to be seriously studied yet.

The next important factor which contributed significantly to rise of population in the Brahmaputra valley are immigrant traders from beyond. The Census of India Report 1901 states, "the immigrants from Rajputana are the shrewd Marwari merchants who have monopolised the trade of the Brahmaputra valley." "Turning to the Asiatic countries beyond India, we find that if we leave Nepal out of consideration, the largest number of immigrants come from Afganistan, 1,101; Burma, 1,666; Bhutan, 919; and Baluchistan, 6,655.[42] The Kabulis are the great pedlars of the province, and come up every year with loads of piece-goods, dry fruits, and similar articles, which they hawk about through the villages and tea gardens but those who were censused in the North Cachar hills were probably serving on the Railways and the same holds good of the natives of Baluchistan."

It is very interesting to note that towards the close of the British rule the immigration of Bhutia, Burmese, Afghan and Baluchi labour had almost ceased though Kabuli pedlars are still found. They had tended to engage themselves in money-lending business in the new urban centres instead of hawking in sundry goods. The task of supplying the needs of the people in all quarters of the province seems to have been monopolized by the "Kayas", that is, the Rajasthani traders, who were now designated by this name by the people of the province.[43]

The decline in the Afghan, Burmese and Bhutia labour immigration may be attributed to political reasons perhaps and the Baluchis might have been absorbed in the Army. But the rise of the Rajasthani traders is quite interesting and needs a little more study to appreciate the cause of its growth. The Rajputs from the time of Akbar the Great had become the bulwark of the Mughal Government and were found employed at all levels of the imperial administration. But when the Mughal Government decayed and Rajputana was rent by successive invasions and expeditions, the Rajputanis found it difficult probably to earn fair living on the arid soils of their land and out of their natural antipathy to foreigners and dependent living took up commerce for living, giving up their traditional trade in arms. Throughout the British regime they are found all over the north as a community of businessmen only; seldom we find anybody going for government service.

The next factor of growth of population in the province is the development of rail transport in the province. Construction of railways in the province began in right earnest after the growth of the plantation industries in Assam. The Assam Railways Trading Company referred to before mainly intended to serve the tea gardens of Upper Assam as was the case with Jorhat State Railways. The development of Railways in Tezpur area was undertaken with a similar view and the connection on Lumding to Badarpur which had already been connected to Chandrapur was undertaken to facilitate the transportation of plantation labour and shipment of Assam Tea via Surma river.

In any case the construction of railway networks throughout the province was completed by the third decade of the present century and Assam had now a good mileage of railways. The railways found it necessary to employ non-Assamese people to run its works. Almost without exception the employees were Bengalis or upcountry men. During the construction period labour was imported from different parts and many Afghan, Baluchi and Nepali labourers were engaged; but on completion the management was left with the Bengalis. The higher posts, however, were retained for the white people.

The railways not only employed for its operation non-Assamese people, the workshops and other offices which were set up in course of time offered many jobs, again to non-Assamese people. In almost all railway offices, the clerical jobs became a monopoly of the Bengalis and lower grade works or labourers were mostly people from Bihar and Uttar Pradesh. The railway workshops similarly depended for labour and office work on non-Assamese people. The transfer of Chandrapur workshop of the Assam Bengal Railways to Dibrugarh caused enmass immigration of Chittagong people who were employed in that workshop to Dibrugarh in 1935.

Besides the railways water transport also offered employment to non-Assamese people. Steamship service which till the close of the 19th century was the only channel of communication of the province practically employed entirely non-Assamese people. The people who served on the ships were recruits of Eastern Bengal; they, of course, did not settle in the province. But those who served at the different ghats or embarcation points and offices and godowns therein were also mostly non-Assamese people

The total of the heads who were serving in the transportation service were enumerated at 69,636 in 1901;[44] the number seems to have declined to 54,974 in 1931.[45] The decline might have been due to retrenchment of the railway labour after the construction of track. The number of persons engaged in transportation service must have increased during the war period but statistics of 1941 census for them are not available.

The provincial government had imported a lot of non-Assamese people into Assam. After the withdrawal of the Army detachments when civil administration was introduced, the British brought in non-Assamese revenue collectors and clerks to serve the government. In course of its long rule, as and when government establishments expanded more and more people were called in. The introduction of district and sub-divisional system of civil administration and Police, establishment of Public Works Department, extension of Postal and Telegraph services, introduction of Health Services and even higher education necessitated the employment of non-Assamese people in the government service. In Assam there was no scope for higher education and technical training and as such higher grades of these services opened to Indians were offered to non-Assamese people. Public Administration offered 17,676 jobs in 1901[46] and the number increased to 100719 in 1931.[47] In government offices also usually non-Assamese people were preferred by many heads of provincial government as they considered them to be more efficient. Many of those who served in government offices, on retirement settled down in the province and thus added to the population of the province.

The Army deployed in Assam consisted of mainly the non-Assamese people. To begin with an attempt was made to recruit t b l people of the province in Sebundy troops deployed as frontier guards. But in course of time policy to recruit Nepalis from Darjeeling was begun.The Assam Rifles who were posted as frontier guards thus became a monopoly of non-Assamese people and after the Mutiny practically no Assamese was recruited in the Indian Army. The people who served in the armed forces of the province totalled 19,576 in 1901[48] and their member rose to 110095 in 1931.[49] Many of these people again on retirement settled down in the province.

Along with the government the Christian Church also contributed to a lesser extent to the growth of population. The number of priests attached to Christian Churches and educational institutions were not many yet they were a powerful and influential community in the new environment of the province and as such deserve special mention.

During the Second Great War a lot of foreign people had come to Assam and after the termination of the war some stayed on. Of those who after the cessation did not go back to their country the Chinese were most numerous and brought in a considerable new element in Upper Assam frontier society.[50] When Kuomintang China was debarred from access to the sea by the Japanese occupation of the coastal region, Chiang Kai-shek who still held "free China" in the south-west lost contact with the western world. A road was hastily built to connect Chunking, the new capital, in the Szechuan province, with Burma to obtain war supplies from the United States.[51] And when the United States joined the war with the Allies and General Still Well took over the command of the North-East India and China, the road link with Burma through Upper Assam was established. A lot of Chinese labour were employed during this last phaze of the war in Upper Assam. On cessation of hostilities, the American soldiers left Upper Assam, but the Chinese labour continued to stay on till many of them were deported during the Sino-Indian border troubles of 1960s.

Besides these imported groups of immigrant population there were many professional groups who had come to settle voluntarily in Assam valley. These were the lawyers and their clerks in the different administrative headquarters, physicians in urban centres, traders from Bengal who had undertaken small-scale shop-keeping business and carpenters and masons, washermen and barbers, fishermen, rickshaw-pullers, etc., all through the province. It may be interesting to note that people from Lower Assam showed a remarkable tendency from the beginning of the present century to migrate to the Darrang and Lakhimpur districts in considerable numbers to take up independent business professions. A considerable quantity of Kamrup people are now found settled in Dum Duma beyond Dibrugarh.

Assam is a land of plenty. When in 1963 I had submitted my resignation in Tura College after serving for about 10 months and was going to join a College in Midnapore district in West Bengal, one of my students remarked, "Sir, nobody after joining service in Assam goes back." I told him that this truth was going to be belived in my case". I was mistaken.

Throughout the British period Assam was, from the economic point of view, a country of prosperity. Its agriculture, though dependent largely on the vagaries of nature, was prosperous after all. No fertilizer was necessary for agriculture; abundant rainfall made irrigation useless. A little soil produced enough food and hardly Assamese cultivators resorted to double cropping. Service or employment in the government agencies was easily available and petty business yielded good income though no social position. Commerce and Industry had tremendous potential which till now requires outlets to flourish. Naturally people could come and easily settle down provided they were determined to withstand the unhealthy climate of the province.

The climate of Assam was a great deterrent to immigration. Malaria, Kala-Azar, Plague, Typhoid, Pneumonia, Dysentery and diarrhoea had much hold over the life of the people. Abundant rainfall and consequent swamps and forests and wilderness made the whole province evergreen paradise of marshes and trees. Mosquitoes and insects, worms and wild animals and snakes were abundant and took a huge toll every year.

LACK OF COMMUNICATION

People coming to Assam were practically lost to their relatives or kinsmen living outside Assam. A journey by rail from Dibrugarh in Upper Assam to Calcutta which was well connected took three days and a terrible river crossing at Pandu. Journey by steamer took seven days and nights. In those days of no air flight, journey to other places was worst and unthinkable. The expenses and journey time and uncertainty naturally held back many industrious people[52]

INHUMAN TREATMENT BY PLANTERS AND INDUSTRIALISTS

The treatment meted out to the tea garden labour and industrial workers and their living conditions compelled many to run away and those who had gone home back somehow naturally prevented many willing immigrants to go to Assam for settlement or employment.

NOTES

1. A Mackenzie, *History of the Relations of the Government with the Hill*
2. Hunter, op.cit. *QSTribes of the North-East Frontier of Bengal*, p. 7.
3. *Assam Administration Report 1874-78,* Part I
4. *Ibid.*
5. *Census of India* 1901
6. W. W. Hunter *Statistical Account of Assam* Vol. I
7. *Assam Administration Report*, 1874-76, Part I.
8. *Census of India Report*, 1901.
9. *Census of India Report*, 1941.
10. Hunter, op. cit. Vol II
11. *Census Report*, 1901.
12. *Ibid*, 1941.
13. *Assam Administration Report*, 1874-76.
14. *Census Report*, 1901, 1941.
15. *Assam Administration Report*, 1874-76, Part I.
16. *Ibid.*
17. *Census Report*. 1901, 1947.
18. *Assam Administration Report*, 1874-76
19. *Census Report*, 1901.
20. *Ibid*., 1941.
21. *Assam Administration Report*, 1874-76. Part I
22. *Census Report*. 1941.
23. *Census Report*. 1901.
24. *Ibid*., 1941.
25. *NEFA - Land and the People*
26. The number of the population of these tribes were not enumerated in census reports properly during the British period.
27. *Ibid.*
28. *Ibid.*
29. *Castes and Tribes* - Tea Districts Labour Association

30. *Tea District Labour Hand Book*
31. *Ibid.*
32. *"Socio-cultural Life of the Tea Garden Labour"*, M. L. Bose, paper presented at a Seminar held at Janata Bhaban, Dishpur, on Problem of Tea India between November 22-23, 1975.
33. *Ibid.*
34. *Census Report*, 1901
35. Study is based on *Census of India Reports* 1881-1931; "Migration of landless labourers from East Bengal to Assam valley" published in *Assam Economic Journal*, Dibrugarh University, in March 1976.
36. *Ibid.*
37. *Ibid.*
38. *Census Report*, 1931.
39. *Census Report*, 1931.
40. D. Wright (ed). *History of Nepal.*
41. D. R. Regme, *Modern Nepal*, Vol II.
42. *Census Report*, 1901.
43. *Ibid.*
44. *Census Report*, 1901.
45. *Ibid.* 1931.
46. *Census Report*, 1901.
47. *Ibid.*, 1931.
48. *Ibid.*
49. *Ibid.*
50. *Census Report*, 1951.
51. H. Vinacka, *A History of the Far East in Modern Times.* (6th Edition, Indian Reprint) p.638.
52. N. Robinson, *A Descriptive Account of Assam.*

SIX

Social Dynamics and Cultural Profile

After the annexation of Assam (1826) by the British the political boundary of Assam underwent several changes and by successive measures contiguous hills and plains were tagged to the province. Naturally the structure of Assamese society changed; a new social fabric of variegated pattern emerged as a result of interplay of new social dynamics. During the British regime (1826-1947) new administrative arrangements were provided and new avenues of employment and occupation were created. The old monarchical officialdom and their offices were no longer there and the British set up, in their place, a new class of officials and establishments. New trading classes, husbandsmen, missionaries and educators began to assume work in the new environment and a new social organization evolved as a result. Homogeneity in Assamese society was lost and the new Assamese society now consisted of Bengali population and up country businessmen, Nepalee husbandsmen, Punjabi soldiers', Afgan traders, Burmese and Bhutia porters and non-Assamese tribal people who were imported to serve in the plantations from outside the province. The population of Assam estimated at 4,132,019 in 1874 came to 75,930,000 in 1941.

TABLE 1: **Religious Distribution of Population of Assam**

Year	Hindu	Muslim	Animistic	Christian	Buddhist	Brahma	Jain	Sikh	Misc
1901	3429033	1581317	1068334	35967	8911	360	1707	505	51
1931	5204650	2780514	992399	249246	15045	included in Hindu	2803	2789	480

Source Census Reports of 1901 and 1931

TABLE 2: **Linguistic Break-up (in thousands)**

Year	Assamese	Bengali	Hindi	Nepali	Others	Total
1901	2120	4382	608	20.2	-	6126
1931	2157	4289	528	88.3	1980	9042

Source: Census Reports of India 190 and 1931

The pre-British Assamese social structure was vertical. At the apex of the structure stood the Ahom monarch and the princes who were hereditary nobles and were highest dignitaries and enjoyed social pre-eminence. They were followed by the counsellors or ministers termed Bor Gohains or Bura Gohains who were also selected from amongst certain specific families.[2] Together with the princes they constituted the upper strata of the Ahom social structure. They enjoyed preference to the rest of the officialdom who were again subdivided into a number of grades according to rank and responsibility. Every individual was an official first in Ahom society and usually paid for his service in land or slave or both. Social privileges and prestige varied according to rank and though to a lesser extent promotion to higher grades was possible, usually society integrated to Ahom structure remained static and birth determined the social status of every individual.[3]

Besides the officialdom there were a few Hindu priests and Ahom priests (Deodhai-Bailungs) and some professional classes like the goldwashers, fishermen and scavengers. The Muslims who had settled down in Assam were engaged in deciphering and interpreting of Persian documents, carving of inscriptions on copper plates and other metals, minting of coins, embroidery work, painting of fast colours, carpentry, sword and gun making and manufacturing of gun powder. There were a few tailors, weavers, braziers and artisans as well. But these professional classes were mere auxiliariea of the Ahom-Assamese society. Slavery in Ahom society was a recognized institution but the position of the slave in society depended much on his or her caste or in other words birth determined slaves' social position.

Thus the Hindu social structure of ancient times was adjusted by the Ahoms to their socio-political requirements. The original Hindu organization of Varna-Asrama concept which dominated the Hindu society or the pre-Ahom society underwent basic changes during the Ahom period. Nevertheless the Ahom society remained by and large homogeneous though the Ahoms inter-married with the tribal people.

By the year 1947 the British Government had set up a comprehensive system of administration which they considered suitable for Assam and a new channel of communication was set up along with new welfare services. The district and sub-divisional system of revenue and judicial administration was set up and to maintain law and order police stations and outposts were established throughout the length and breadth of the country. Local Boards and Town Committees were set up to carry on the local administration in rural and urban centres respectively. Postal services and telegraph lines, hospitals and charitable dispensaries were established. Steamers and railways provided new arteries of communication. Schools and colleges were created to provide new education to the new generation.[4] Employment in Government service now was thrown open to any and everyone and merit and efficiency were the only considerations by and large. Birth or caste had no consideration to employment till the latter phase of the British raj when reservations were made for very many considerations. The people employed in these services emerged in society as a new class of people composed of different castes and creeds.

Education is the only single factor which more than any other contributes to the change in society. Education inculcates liberal progressive ideas into the minds of people and thus prepares them for reorganization and reforms in society. The British had established their sway over the region as early as the beginning of the second quarter of the 19th century; but English education did not make much of a progress till the end of the century. At the close of the century there were only 20 English High Schools, five of which were aided and five were run on public charity, only 10 being run by the Government. There were two colleges at the beginning of the present century and there was no technical college or college for medicine.[4]

But the people of Assam had realized the necessity and implication of western education. The efforts of the people and their pressure on the Administration resulted in an increase of educational institutions in the province.

The statistics of the year 1947-48 show that the number of primary schools rose to 7,374, with an enrolment of 393,247 pupils in them; the number of High Schools rose to 191 with an enrolment of 68,762; and the number of colleges rose to 18 of which some were professional colleges. There was now an Engineering and Technological Institute and a School for Medicine as well.[5]

The new education provided by the English added a new dimension in society. A class of pupils hitherto unknown emerged in society and they were headed by a class of professional teachers. Both the teachers and students were new classes composed of different castes and creeds and yet enjoyed much prestige in society.

The development of education had also created a market for newspapers, magazines and reading materials for general people. A new class of writers of text-books, general books, litterateurs had also emerged in society. Subsidiary to these were a class of people who depended on these educational institutions for their subsistence. A large number of book-sellers and suppliers of stationery and sundry other items which these institutions required were supplied by many.

In the realm of economy a new kind of enterprises began to be founded. Factories and plantations, oil-fields and coal-mines, shops and bazars were established all through the country. Tea industry started in the thirties of the 18th century had, at the time of independence, become by far the largest single factor in the new economy of the country. The area under cultivation rose to 309 kh. of 998 gardens in 1946 and 954,000 labourers were employed in 1941 in them.[7] Petroleum, discovered in 1825, by 1942 became a prosperous industry in Digboi of Upper Assam where a beautiful township had grown up. Coal-mines were worked in Lakhimpur district in the neighbourhood of Digboi and also in the Khasi-Jaintia hills. New industrial and commercial enterprises created new conditions and generated a new class of big businessmen and industrialists or planters who swelled the bourgeois rank. A class of labourers who were completely dependent on their wages for their subsistence, a phenomenon entirely new in the history of the region, emerged in the economy of the province.

In the economic set-up the garden managers or refinery or coal-mine managers with their assistants stood at the apex. They were usually Europeans and enjoyed highest position in the country. Next to them were the physicians and office assistants and technicians who were usually Indians and were known as middle-class people. They were followed by labourers who were by far the most numerous section and constituted the lowest strata in the new society. The new occupational groups were caste-less people, for caste had no role to play in shaping the economic behaviour of the people now.

The rural economy also underwent a change. Now land revenue had to be paid in money and there was no limitation on the possession of land by an individual; one could take up as much land as one could manage to cultivate and pay revenue. The abolition of slavery put a restraint on the former aristocracy and the industrious peasants amassing wealth became the "Yeoman" in rural society. No longer official ranks determined social status or comforts. New village heads and Mauzadars who were recognized and employed by the Government were not necessarily people of former aristocratic class. These new office holders emerged as leaders in rural areas and became the stalwarts of rural society.

The growth of towns and bazars was a new phenomena in Assamese society. Of course Gauhati and Goalpara had begun to evolve as urban centres even before Assam was annexed in 1826. But in the new district or sub-divisional headquarters of the province population grew and daily bazars developed there. The people who served in the offices, lawyers, doctors, school-teachers, shop-keepers and tradesmen (and a host of other professional groups*) settled in them. In course of time these developed into towns and a class of town dwelling people began to emerge in society. Setting up of schools and other educational institutions in them attracted people from the rural areas to come and settle in them. The number of towns rose to 30 in 1947 and urban population rose to 315,917 in

1931.[8] The population in these towns became little more alert and conscious than the people of the rural areas and naturally these people became the spokesmen of the country. But it should be remembered that the population of the urban centres was mixed and the majority were non-Assamese office workers, professional men or traders or husbandsmen.

TABLE 3: **Industrial and Plantation Population (in thousands)**

Year	Tea	Petrolium	Coal
1901	653.5	-	
1931	1076.1	8.8	7.3

Source: Census Reports of 1901 and 1931

TABLE 4: **Professional Break-up**

Profession	Year 1901	Year 1931
Public Administration	17676	10719
Profession and Liberal Arts	75126	43109
Law and Clerks	3160	-
Medicine	8966	-
Letters, Arts and Science	7962	10561
Public Force	19576	11095
Mines (Coal and Petroleum)	3495	16525
Industry*	200284	323949
Transport	69636	54974
Trade	247462	120748

***Industry** Basketry
Cotton
Pottery
Rice plantation
Silk
Tailors

Source Census Reports of 1901 and 1931

Another factor that contributed to the change of social structure to a great extent was proselitisation. With the establishment of the British regime Christian missionaries of different churches came to Assam and though their efforts to convert the plains people practically failed they succeeded in course of time to convert a considerable section of the tribal population. Not only a new class of ecclesiastics came into existence in the several churches established in Assam but a new community of alien religious profession was now added to the social structure. As a result of these proselytizing activities, Indian reformists and missionaries began to set up religio-cultural centres in Assam and a new class of monastics, distinct from the former priesthood, emerged in society. Sri Rama Krishna Mission, the Brahmo Samaj, the Arya Samaj, the Theosophical Society, the Muslim organizations began to be set up. The Hindu and Buddhist temples together with the Satras and mosques of former times, of course, continued to exist with their theologians. The people engaged in the new monasteries constituted yet another class in society.

Thus as a result of the impact of the British raj we find an altogether new social organization in Assam when India became independent in 1947. The Assamese society which was more or less homogeneous and vertical in structure became heterogeneous in composition and horizontal in structure. The Government high officials, tea garden managers and business managers of oil and other industries, who were usually Europeans, together with the Christian missionaries, constituted the canopy of the new Anglo-Indian society.

Next were a professional class of lawyers and physicians and high Indian officials and owners of tea gardens who constituted the second class of people in the new social structure. They were followed by college and school-teachers and lesser officials including the clerks, typists, etc., of government offices and people employed in transport, postal and charitable institutions. The new ecclesiastic of Sri Rama Krishna Mission, the Brahmo Samaj, the Arya Samaj, the Theosophical Society, and Maulanas supplemented these indigenous aristocrats. Parallel to them were the Mouzadars, Gaorburas and wealthy peasants in the rural areas, the priests attached to temples or Mullas attached to the mosques and madrassas or maqtabs, and the traders and businessmen. These classes of people in course of time began to be known as the middle classes. The next class was constituted by the peasants and the fourth grade office employees or peons. And at the lowest rung of the social structure remained the tea garden labourers and labourers in oil and coal industries or porters of railway and steamer services.

It can be assumed, perhaps, without the risk of oversimplification that the society created by the British was modelled on the English pattern. At the top rung of the social ladder was a small contingent of European "colons"; below them were the bourgeois or middle class lawyers, doctors, few well-to-do planters and ryots, officials and tradesmen; next were the peasantry who were followed by the labouring class. The beaurucratic government of the Anglo-Indian thrived on the support and assistance of the bourgeois class and allowed it to grow. But the natural sovereigns of the country and aristocracy of former days became disorganized and helpless and so also was the case with the peasantry and labour.

CULTURAL PROFILE

The new social structure of the British regime upheld a new variegated pattern of culture. It was a synthesis of the renaissance Bengali, European, rather Victorian British, and traditional Assamese culture with a slight mixture of Hindustani. It has to be remembered that the traditional Assamese culture was a composite one which was a product of the interaction of tribal or Indo-Mongoloid and Indo-Aryan or Hindu culture. But Assam had now become politically a mosaic of several tribal tracts or hills each with a separate way of life and the two valleys of the Barak and the Brahmaputra inhabited predominantly by the Bangalis and Assamese respectively. In the Brahmaputra valley, now, a considerable Bengali population settled down; these people together with the traders of Rajasthan and non-Assamese tribal plantation labour added colours to the existing mosaic of Assamese culture.

The new townships which sustained the new culture sprang up around the offices of the provincial, district and sub-divisional headquarters spontaneously. In 1901, there were some 18 towns in Assam and the population in them totalled 187,162 (including Manipur) which was over 2.9 per cent of the total of the province.[9] Of these none was of commercial importance. But by 1931 the number of townships rose to 30 and the population in them rose to 315,917 which was three per cent of the provincial total.[10] Of these Tinsukia was a commercial-cum-railway township. Lumding, a railway junction, was fast growing into a town towards the close of British rule.

The growth of the townships offers almost a uniform pattern of development. To begin with, accommodation was provided for residential purpose by the Government only to the European staff and gradually as more houses were built quarters were provided to senior staff members of the offices. Therefore others were required to either rent a house or build one for their own accommodation. So houses near the office buildings began to be set up. The people coming to these offices required food and shelter, therefore, hotels, teashops, sweet-meat shops and other shops were opened near these offices. Residential quarters were usually named after the mouza or local name but in many places they were named by the nature of its settlement. For example, the area inhabited by clerks was styled Amolapatty, as the clerk in early days was called Omlah. The hangman's place in Gauhati near the prison became famous by the name of Fanci Bazar.

Schools and colleges were set up as per the requirements of a particular locality and availability of land, for though there was plenty of land in Assam, area fit for building houses in the town areas was by no means abundant. Almost all towns sprang up in lowland interposed by ditches and sometimes hillocks. Better sites were kept by the Government for official requirements and the rest was occupied by the rich people. These were nearer to the residential quarters of top officials. In Gauhati, Tezpur and Dibrugarh, for example, the D.C.'s office, residence of the district level officers, Circuit House and the courts, are all situated on the Brahmaputra in the centre of the town. The poor people went away from the centre of these towns but shops were usually set up along the roads of the central place of the townships. The shop-keepers had to stay away from their home for business purposes. Only rich merchants could afford to purchase land near the central place and could accommodate their families and shops within the same premises. Naturally such towns were haphazard growths every where in Assam and show almost the same patterns of developments.

With the progress of time and growth of population, the problems of sanitation, sewage, maintenance of road and lighting developed. So Town Committees and Municipalities began to be created. The government passed Acts for such purposes. Before 1874 when Assam was made a Chief Commissionership there was only one Municipality at Gauhati constituted under the District Towns Improvement Act, 1864, and there were voluntary associations in Tezpur, Sibsagar, Jorhat, Golaghat, Nowgong and Dibrugarh.[11] But after 1874 there was steady growth of local self-government in urban areas. By 1947 there were some 28 urban self-governments set up in several new towns which had come up during the British regime. These were run under provisions of Act V of 1864.[12] This Bengal Act was amended in subsequent years till in 1923 the Government of Assam passed its Municipal Act. Till that time Bengal Act II of 1896 provided the basis of urban self-government in Assam.[13]

The housing problems and unsystematic growth were the common feature in new urban centres of Assam. But in the tea gardens and industrial areas the companies built the quarters required for their employees. These usually centred round the factories of the different companies. There usually an area was earmarked for each category of employee and each class lived a segregated life. The problems of sanitation and education in these were tackled by the respective companies, though the government supervised these aspects of life in these areas. Besides these centres of the new society railways and steamer routes necessitated the growth of a few small clustered residential areas. At big junctions or town railway stations and important steamer ghats small townships developed.

The family structure in these towns usually was of the nuclear type. The service holders or professional men or businessmen lived in towns with their families. Dependants or students related to such a householder sometimes lived with them but their utility in such a family was a potent cause for which they were sheltered. As a rule the joint family system did not obtain in towns. It continued to languish in rural areas.

The traditional housing pattern of Assam underwent a fundamental change in these towns of Assam. The Ahom was accustomed to thatched houses made of bamboo, wood, mud and grass or leaves.[14] Brick-work was confined to the royal palace and temples were built of stone or brick. The new rulers of the province introduced new styles of house building. The bungalows of the high officials or managers of tea estates or coal or petroleum industries were massive, commodious structures raised on high platforms and built of panel wood. The roofs in the initial stages were made either of grass or corrugated iron sheets which were covered with grass to keep them cool during the summer season. The bungalows were provided with attached sanitary latrines and bathrooms with bath-tubs and European style fittings. The inner apartments of the houses were furnished in the European style; carpets, landscapes scenery of the Western countries, bookcases, etc., were nicely placed in the living room. The reception or the drawing room in each bungalow usually contained a fireplace made after the Western fashion, comfortable sofa sets and chairs with a small secretariat table for writing. The walls again were decorated with selected Western landscape scenes or pictures of Kings and Queens of the British Empire. In between the drawing room and the living apartment there was a dining space or room where usually breakfast, lunch and dinner were served. The bungalows were surrounded by a beautifully laid garden, built over a large spacious campus. Sometimes swimming pools or tennis courts were set within the campus and flower beds where flowers of European varieties were carefully grown through the year. In building office houses free use of new materials like corrugated iron sheets, wood, bricks, cement, lime, etc. was made.

The houses of the native officials and new professional classes in urban centres usually were designed after the bungalows. The pattern and area of the residence differed in size and area but the materials used for construction and layout of the house and interior arrangements and fittings were almost similar. The decoration of the house underwent a change with the march of time. Tribal artefacts and Assamese "Jhapi" began to be placed within the drawing rooms of the new bourgeoisie in imitation of the Europeans. Thatched houses continued to be constructed but the design underwent a change and doors and windows were now common in all types of houses and these began to be covered with curtains.

Along with the housing pattern new furniture made its appearance. Bed-steads, cots, chairs and tables became common items in new houses. In the clothing pattern also new styles emerged in keeping with the new furniture. In schools and offices employees and students began to wear trousers and shirts; dhoti and wrappers were used at home but their use in public life was restored only after the *swadeshi* movement gained popularity. Womenfolk and girls began to be clad in saris and frocks and use of blouses and undergarments became quite common. Use of imported toilet soaps, powders, cosmetics were common and bangles and ornaments of new design now are preferred to traditional Assamese varieties. Utensils of newer varieties and metals like frying pans of iron, porcelain dishes and cups entered the new households.

The dietary and their timings were also changed. The Assamese people were accustomed to taking noonday meal and dinner with little vegetables or fish or meat with sufficient quantity of rice. The use of mustard oil and spices was negligible. A popular item was sour soup prepared from a variety of ingredients. But now the officegoers and students had to take their food before 10 and as they were busy in the evening with either reading or marketing or social visits, the evening meal time was pushed back a little. The simple items of dietary were enriched in the Bengali fashion and more items were added to meals. Tea and bakery products found favour in urban households. Tinned food, biscuits, confectionary gained popularity and people evinced more interest in them than in homemade sweets and "pithas". Fruits taken unconscious of their food value before now gained popularity in well-to-do families.

During the British regime new games and sports and pastimes and recreations came into vogue. Football, volleyball, basketball, tennis, badminton, cards, chess, billiards, caromme, etc., became quite popular in Assam. Physical training and atheletics or gymnasium exercise became part of the school education. The old-time pastime of enjoying bull fights or cockfights remained confined to some rural areas but occasionally these were organized in fairs or marketplaces. Club life for the upper strata of society had become quite common and in many such clubs tournaments of indoor and outdoor games were arranged. These clubs introduced amateur dramas and provided recreation to masses till talkie shows in cinema houses became common source of pleasure. Libraries and reading rooms appeared in almost all towns besides being attached to all academic institutions. The number of books published and journals increased considerably; non-secular reading habit exhibited remarkable progress in Assam

A few words may be said here regarding the old temples, Namghars and mosques. In mediaeval times these institutions were centres of cultural and academic life of the people. They provided education and recreation and organized cultural shows and festivals. The place of these was occupied in the new society by the clubs which provided a common meeting ground for all sorts of people. The European clubs were meant exclusively for white people who drank, danced and played among themselves in their clubs. But Indian clubs were open to all linguistic and cultural groups of Indian population. In these clubs a good deal of understanding and exchange of ideas and institutions took place. These clubs sometimes invited professional "Jatra" parties from Calcutta.

The social functions and ceremonies changed their outward observances considerably and some new social ceremonies crept into the society. Birthdays, marriage anniversaries, farewells to parting persons in imitation of the Christians became quite common in the upper classes. For a marriage ceremony now new items were provided to the guests in a well-decorated pandal specially erected for the purpose. A magnificent gate to welcome the guests was erected. For celebrating a birthday, a birthday cake was prepared to add to the solemnity of the occasion.

In the sphere of public life new avenues of recreation were added. The hoary functions of Bihu organized during mid-April and January continued to be celebrated in rural areas but much enthusiasm was evinced in organizing Durga Puja and Kali Puja or Dewali, Saraswati Puja and Holi (Doljatra) festivals in towns. Almost in all towns these were celebrated with pomp and splendour and people eagerly awaited them. A spectacular festival was the immersion ceremony arranged at Dibrugarh. All images of Durga from the neighbouring tea gardens between Tinsukia and Dibrugarh were brought to Dibrugarh by a special train of open wagons and a great fair was organized at Dibrugarh. The images were immeresed in the Brahmputra in the presence of a huge crowd of enthusiastic onlookers. In the new religious institutions like the Brahmasabha, Sri Ramkrishna Mission or Arya Sabha people gathered in the evening to join in worship or listen to religious discourses. Every Sunday the Christians assembled in the Church for the service. The Christians looked for Christmas when the Churches and houses were tastefully decorated for the occasion. The garden labour added new social functions like Karma Puja. Going for a picnic during the winter season became a general practice among the people of the new society in the towns. Gramophone provided recreation in many rich urban families. Cinema houses began to provide recreation to people from the thirties of the present century and towards the close of the British regime all important district headquarters had at least one talkie cinema house.

The moral tone of the new generation was positively on the lower side. The decadence of the Ahom rule had brought to the country a period of chaos and confusion which resulted in an increase in crime, rapine and moral degeneration which the Europeans have amplified in their accounts of the 19th Century. During the British regime brothels as recognized institutions usually developed in all the new towns and concubinage among the officials and professional people was quite a common thing. A man's status in society sometimes was determined by the number of his concubines. But monogamy had become the general rule in town families and opium eating progressively decreased. Addiction to wine and gambling and smoking of cigaraters were common among the town people but truthfulness, sanctity of promises and piety, among the people, were quite remarkable.

In spite of these new tendencies in towns, it must be said that the different tribes of the province in their respective hills and people in rural areas in both the valleys continued to live their traditional life by and large. Of course the new ideas and improvements in many ways began to inflitrate into the rural settings and tribal villages. Nevertheless the rustics remained wedded to their ancestral practice of production and construction and social habits and customs.

NOTES

1. A sizable Punjabi population has settled all over Assam.
2. Wade, op. cit., pp. VI-X.
3. Hamilton, op. Cit. pp., 18-24.
4. Census Reports, 1901, 1911, 1921, 1931.
5. *Census Report, 1901.*
6. *Statistical HandBook of Assam.*
7. Ibid.

8. *Census Report, 1931.*
9. *Census Report, 1901.*
10. *Census of India Report, 1931.*
11. *V. Venkata Rao. Hindred years of Local Self-Government*
12. Ibid
13. Ibid
14. John M. Cosh. Topography of Assam *p. 27*

SEVEN

The Genesis of Ethnic Identity and Social Tension

The civilization that flourished in North-Eastern India was an integral part of the Indo-Aryan civilization of India; Hindu civilization here in this region was a cohesive force that united and bound the Austro-Dravidian, Indo-Tibetan and Indo-Aryan races; and this civilization generated an air of mutual give-and-take, amity and prosperity. The virility of the new people found expression in the Kamrup Kingdom of Vaskara Varma the testimony of which is found in the accounts of Hiuen-Tsang; unfortunately the history of the post-Vaskara period of Kamrupa is in the womb of oblivion. Thanks to the prowess and sagacity of the Ahoms, Assam once again emerged as one of the premier kingdoms of India out of the debris of political disintegration and chaos which followed disintegration of Kamrupa.

In the historical literature of pre-British times not a single reference to any ethnic rivalry or racial riot or hill-plains discord is found; from the pre-historic period Mongoloid, Austric and Caucasian and Alpine people fused themselves to form one people. Muslims who settled in Assam during the mediaeval period were absorbed within the Assamese community as were the Bengalis who had been coming from time to time from the adjacent territories of Bengal. The different Indo-Tibetan people had no complaint against the Indo-Aryan settlers who are regarded as Assamese in the plains. Yet a specious but hollow theory has been carefully and deliberately built up to make people believe that the British had brought the diverse people of the hills and plains under one single administration and thus gave them a chance to live in unity and harmony and foster common political and cultural bonds of union.

When Assam was annexed to the British territories after the first Anglo-Burmese War (1824-25), the English had to, recruit a number of Bengali employees in different offices of the new administration of Assam. The education of the Assamese youth of that time did not warrant their employment under the British Government.[1] Therefore in offices Bengalis were posted and in the Army and irregular forces non-Assamese tribals and upcountry people or Gorkhas were employed. With the progress of new education in the province Assamese youth aspired for employment. But already a large number of Bengalis had been imported to serve the Administration and their successors now grew in number and thwarted the ambition of the Assamese youth. Around the sub-divisional and district courts a large number of lawyers and their clerks were established. In these also the Assamese intelligensia lagged behind the Bengalis. As there was no technical and professional college in Assam till the late years of the British Raj, it was difficult for an average Assamese to proceed beyond Assam to receive such education. As a corollary to such a situation the leaders of society began to mobilize public opinion and request the authorities for reservation of employment for Assamese youth and this kept up a spirit of animosity against the Bengalis.[2]

The economy of Assam, we have seen already, had undergone revolutionary changes. The tea plantations, oil and coal industries and the new markets that grew up in the new urban centres provided liveli-hood to, the multitudes. But in these practically no indigenous people were absorbed. In the plantations labour was imported from outside; clerical and technical hands were recruited from Bengal or from among the Bengalis of Assam and the case in the oil industry and coal mines was similar. Trade and commerce had been monopolized by the people of Rajasthan and cattle farming and dairy industry were controlled by the Nepalees. Fish and vegetable market went under the control of the Hindustanis. In fact the new economy did not provide any opportunity to the Assamese youth. The large income from plantations and industries went to enrich the British merchants as the economy was colonial in character. The people of

Assam thinned by civil strife and Burmese wars found engagement only in the agricultural sector and till that sector could provide them, subsistence there was no social tension in spite of repeated provocation from the Press and platform.

Education in Assam had progressed at very slow rate. Neither good institutions nor efficient teachers were available. The inadequacy of textbook, and long distances that the students were required to travel to attend educational institutions did not provide much impetus to acquire education. The contents of the books did not envisage the production of patriotic liberal minded citizens, with a wide nationalistic outlook. It has been very aptly pointed out that the aim of the English to educate the Indians was either to produce caricatures of European characters who would be willing to accept the gospel of Christ or to get a regular supply of cheap clerks to serve them in the business organizations of the Government of India and subsidiary undertakings of the British subjects.[3] Hence with the exception of a few, the English educated youth looked for employment with the Government or merchant farms to live a European style of life. Those who did not get any such opportunity looked for causes of their misery and found out that if the supply were less and competition nil they could have got employment as alternatives.

At the beginning of the British rule in Assam, though there was a little awareness among the people that the Bengalis were monopolizing the employment in the new Government, the newly educated people had shown a predilection for Bengali culture. People returning from Bengal after education had accepted many Bengali ways and initiated a movement for reforms in lines of Bengal.[4] But the language issue created an antagonism between the Assamese and Bengalis permanently. The exchange of arguments and counter-arguments to prove that Assamese was a separate language and not a corrupt dialect of the Bengali embittered the relations between the two communities. The Assamese intelligentsia who had initiated a cultural synthesis were turned into leaders of an anti-Bengali movement putting a halt on the assimilation.

The Sepoy Mutiny and setting of Bahadur Shah on the throne of Delhi had showed the unpopularity and shaky foundation of the Company's empire in India and the unity of the diverse communities in opposing the alien rule. And the disclosure of the intrigues of Maniram Dewan against the British Raj made the rulers to devise what is popularly known as divide-and-rule policy. The Assamese people in general had practically shown no sympathy for the mutineers and soon after the assumption of power by the British Crown steps began to be taken for the separation of Assam from Bengal. The Assamese language which was suspended from office and school was reintroduced in the official and educational use in 1873 and in 1874 Assam was constituted into a separate Administration.

The use of Bengali as the language of the court and educational institutions had done great harm to the people of Assam and driven a permanent wedge between the two communities of Assamese and Bengalis. As a result of use of Bengali between 1837 and 1873 as the medium of instruction, education of the Assamese could not progress and a lot of Bengalis were imported and employed in the different schools of Assam. Writing of text books in Assamese for school children in Assamese did not get any encouragement and Assamese literature naturally suffered in its growth. The enmity between the two linguistic groups that was created was never completely obliterated.

The reason shown for the separation of Assam was strategic.[5] But the annexation of Cachar and Sylhet to the Assam Commission was purposive. The reason shown was economic rather then administrative; the surplus revenue of the Surma Valley was to balance the deficit in the valley of the Brahmaputra.[6] But the members of the Viceroy's Council had written in the minutes that Assam under the Central Government would enjoy both encouragement and financial support. And in any case all expenditure came from the common purse and all excess would pour in the central exchequer. Therefore monetary considerations seem to be untenable. Administratively, the Surma Valley, particularly Sylhet, was regulation district under permanent settlement and under the jurisdiction of the High Court of Calcutta: it had no administrative similarity with Assam. The people of Sylhet had also submitted a "memorial" to the governor-General opposing the amalgamation with Assam with which country they had no similarity social or linguistic.[7] But the prospect of monopoly of jobs in the new province brought the opposition to naught and further the form of administration was not affected in any way by the attachment of the district to the Assam Administration.

But the seeds of Assamese and Bengali communal jealousy and rivalry were firmly sown now. In the new capital of the province in a tribal territory the people of the Surma Valley monopolized the jobs in the Chief Commissioner's establishment and it was not till the 20th century that they faced any serious opposition from the educated tribal people. But it was in the administrative centres within the plain districts that the rivalry and jealousy became ripe. Some Bengalis adopted a haughty attitude following their English masters who deliberately fostered such an outlook and thus antagonized the Assamese people.

The communal feeling which had been simmering burst forth at the time of partition of Bengal in 1905.[8] The Assam Association and its branches everywhere protested against the proposed merger of Assam with Eastern Bengal. They had expressed their apprehension of being overwhelmed and absorbed by the Bengali people. The Gouripur Branch of the Assam Association had suggested that in the event of any enlargement of territory of the province of Assam, Cooch-Behar, Rangpur, Dinajpur, Jalpaiguri and Bogra districts of North Bengal might be attached to Assam for the Assamese people had much affinity, both linguistic and cultural with the people of these districts.[9] They still cherished the cultural unity of North-Eastern India.

But then the amalgamation of these districts would strengthen the new province and the scheme of dividing the communities and thus sapping their virility would fail. The amalgamation of Assam with Eastern Bengal would serve the double purpose of dividing the Bengali community politically and on the basis of religion. In the new province of Eastern Bengal and Assam, the Bengali Hindus would be a minority, and pro-British Mahammadans would cooperate with the Government.[10] Secondly, the new province would suffer from Assamese-Bengali rivalry and jealousy. Therefore Assam was amalgamated with Eastern Bengal and thus the double mischief of communal and linguistic dissensions was set afoot.

However, Assam was separated from Eastern Bengal in 1912 and again a Chief Commissionership was created for its administration. But the temporary amalgamation had embittered the race relations to a great extent. Though there was a general sympathy of the educated Assamese for the divided Bengalis and the Swadeshi and Boycott movements gained much popularity in Assam, the intelligentsia were becoming uneasy at the increase of the number of Bengalis in Government employment.[11] Moreover the Mahammadans of Sylhet under the influence of the Muslim League backed by the Government now began to become anti-Hindu.[12] What was worst was that the Mahesyas of Sylhet directly opposed the move of the Indian National Congress which they considered to be a caste Hindu organization.[13] Further at the restoration of Sylhet to the Assam Administration, the dormant Bengali antipathy for living within Assam was again roused and a movement for secession from Assam ensued.

The movement for reunion of Sylhet which started immediately after the restoration of the Assam Chief Commissionership was initiated by the Muslim population of Sylhet.[14] It was a Muslim majority Bengali-speaking district. The move to unite with the East Bengal Muslims was supported by the Muslims of Dacca on emotional grounds. But very soon on political considerations the Muslims of Dacca as well as Sylhet gave up the demand. The Hindus of Sylhet, however, carried on the secessionist movement subsequently till the end of the British regime as they considered that they had no affinity whatsoever to the Assamese in geographical, linguistic and ethnological aspects.[15] The demand, ignored by the Government, became alive again when the Monteford Reform Scheme came up for discussion.

In fact the people of Sylhet had acquired a predominant position in the Assam Administration. But as proposals came up for setting up a High Court and University for Assam, it was apprehended by the people of the Surma Valley that these would be set up in the Brahmaputra Valley and would thus put them in a backward position, rather the people of Assam valley would derive more benefit. The Assamese people, however, considered that the separation of Sylhet with Bengali Muslim majority population would be a blessing for them as such supported their demand. In 1947 when a referendum was held in sylhet the Hindus voted for incorporation of Sylhet in Assam but the Muslims voted in favour of Pakistan. The Muslims of the Brahmputra valley however desired the inclusion of Sylhet in Assam.

Meanwhile the Sylhet Bengali secessionist movement had started a similar very vigorous movement in the Bengali speaking population of the border district of Goalpara in the Brahmaputra valley. The intelligentsia of Goalpara district were Bengali and the Zamindars held permanent settlement under Lord Cornwallis' Act of 1793. Their estate interests were identical with those of their counterparts of Bengal. Therefore following the secessionist move in 1912 in Sylhet they launched a movement for reunion with Bengal. Their movement too became dormant when the Government declared its decision not to transfer any territory of Assam Chief Commissionership to Bengal.[16] But when Lord Chelmsford proposed reforms in the Indian Administration, together with the people of Sylhet, Goalpara intelligentsia demanded incorporation of Goalpara district in the province of Bengal.

The secessionist movement in Goalpara roused the Assamese intelligentsia of the Brahmaputra valley to the danger of territorial loss. Though the demand of the people of Sylhet was supported, the move of the Bengali people of Goalpara was condemned. A sequal of this movement and counter movement resulted in strained relations between the two linguistic communities and both looked back to trace a separate ethnic origin and identity.

To use the Mahammadans against the Hindus, the Mahammadans were given favour and their communal organizations encouraged. The Muslim League was born with the blessings of the Government. The partition of Bengal and creation of Eastern Bengal and Assam encouraged Muslim fanaticism and roused Hindu-Muslim suspicion and jealousy. It was held that the new State was created with a view to giving the Muslim community a clear majority and predominant influence in the politics of the new province. The activities of the Anjumans in the Surma Valley and Assam Districts began to disturb the relations between the Hindus and Muslims. The Muslims who had joined the Bengali Hindus of Sylhet in opposing the merger of Assam with East Bengal soon changed sides and backed the Government action.[17] After the restoration of the Chief Commissionership of Assam Muslims were given representation in the Legislative Assembly. Bengali "colonists", as the Muslim immigrants from Bengal were called, continued to pour into Assam. The Muslim population of Assam in 1911 was 355, 320 but it rose to 1,305, 902 in 1941.[18]

These immigrants spurred the Assamese-Bengali antagonism. When the people of Assam were being "swamped" by these waves of immigration, the leaders of this group began to hold communal meetings and some of their leaders began to assert that "to ask a Bengali to give up his mother tongue and inherited culture, of which he is as much proud as an Assamese of his own, in exchange for a patch of land-to which he is as much entitled as an Assamese is to ask him to barter away his birth right for mere mess of pottage.[19] This created racial antagonism and stood as an impediment to the growth of friendly relations between the two races which the Muslim leaders professed to remove by abolishing restrictions on immigration in Assam. The Hindu-Muslim amity in Assam was also disturbed by the deliberate attempt to make Assam a Muslim majority State.

A conspicuous achievement of the British regime in Assam was the segregation of the Ahoms from the Assamese community. The Ahoms who trace their descent from the Shan tribe that crossed into the Assam valley in A.D. 1226 had identified themselves with the Assamese. Till 1892 there was no distinction between an Ahom and an Assamese who traced their descent from the pre-Ahom, settlers of Assam; the Ahoms were as good Hindu Assamese as any other of the valley of the Brahmaputra and there was no social barrier between the two; their social system, religion, language and culture were practically one and the same and in the pre-British period they were the elites in Assamese society. In 1893 an Ahom Association was founded to ameliorate the social and economic condition of those who traced their descent from the Shan tribe.[20] The Government viewed with satisfaction the separative tendency and in 1912 two members designated as representatives of the Ahom community were taken in the Assam Legislature.[21] The Government patronage now encouraged the Ahom Association leaders to describe the Congress as a caste Hindu organization and they represented for recognition as a minority community to be kept under the special responsibility of the Governor of Assam. The Communal award of 1935 derecognized the Ahoms as minority community which stiffened the attitude of the Ahom leaders. Some of them moved several resolutions in the State Legislature urging the Government of Assam to move the Union Government for recognition of the Ahoms as a minority community but to no effect. This created antagonism between section of the Ahom community and the rest of the Assamese people.

Meanwhile to divide the Hindu society into segments steps had begun to be taken. As early as 1807 the Court of Directors of the East India Company issued instructions to its government of India to prepare accounts of the different ethnic, linguistic, caste and religious groups.[22] The instructions were faithfully carried out by the servants of the Company in India. Hamilton and Pemberton's **Survey of the North East Frontier of Bengal**, Dalton's **Descriptive Ethnology**, Grierson's **Linguistic Survey of India**, Census Reports from 1881 onwards provide much information regarding the people but the stress on separateness of each linguistic, racial, religious and caste group facilitated the growth of identity of the people with a particular group and thus paved the way for the division of society. These informations were later on utilized as the basis of preparation of the scheduled castes and tribes distinct from the Hindu society of which these tribes and castes were an integral part. Though the myths of purity of race had long been exploded and rejected these scheduled castes and tribes were declared to be of non-Aryan origin and distinct from the caste Hindu society.

The Census of India Report of 1931 writes an interesting note on the caste consciousness of the lower stratum of the Hindu society. The different lower caste people like the Naths, Yogis, Kaivartas, Das, Patnis, Malis and Malakars made attempts to find their glorious origin from the Puranic evidences and change their caste appellation by better or honourable ones. People of these castes now refused to dine with people of higher castes. While the Swadeshi movement launched an attack on the age-old caste system, untouchability, and initiated reforms to remove restrictions on the free movement of women and widow remarriage, the members of the newly awakened hitherto depressed lower classes embarked upon a movement of restricting the movements of women of their class and put a halt to widow remarriage.[23] The people of these castes organized themselves into several social organizations, held regular meetings and annual conferences and attempted to preserve and acquire caste privileges, to raise the status, of their respective castes in relation to other castes, to encourage education among their members, to improve their economic conditions and demand scholarships, special representation in Government services and political institutions. Some such caste organizations even deprecated the Nationalist movement and supported Government repressive measures.

Besides the Government had begun to create a wall of separation between the hill tribes and plains people. To impoverish the hill tribes their lands and forests were attached to British possession and commercial facilities were curtailed; they were pushed inside the rugged mountains. In desperation they were made to raid the plains people. In the name of warding off marauding raids of these people now restrictions on trade, commerce and travel between hills and plains were imposed by issuing the Inner Line Regulation in 1873. The hills people were told that the plains people were exploiting them, whereas the fact was that they had exploited their simplicity and impoverished them in their own hills.

A classic example of the divide-and-rule policy of the British Government in relation to the hill tribes and plains people is found in the change of attitude of the British officers. The Chief Commissioner of Assam proposed measures for better administration of the Naga Hills in 1886 but the Government of India negatived the proposal by stating that "in course of years it will be the ultimate result of our contact with the adjacent tribes is probably certain, but the Government of India have no desire to hasten such a consummation.[24] Even in 1931 the officers in service in the tribal areas held that the progressive absorption (of hill areas) into the province of Assam in the past was forced upon the Government by the unavoidable necessity of securing from the marauding and revengeful raids of its denezens the safety of the plains districts for which the Government had made itself responsible." But the same Government, with the intensification of the Nationalist Movement in India, stood forth as champions of the cause of the simple folk of the hills. In the Census Report of Naga Hills, 1921, J. P. Hulton vivified the exploitation of the Naga people by the plains people, though the Government itself was responsible for it.

Be that as it may, the intelligent emergent leaders of the hill tribes were made anti-Indian by official propaganda and encouragement. As early as 1918 a Naga Club was organized in Kohima to uphold the Naga cause.[25] They began to consider that they would rather remain under the jurisdiction of the British Government instead of being placed at the disposal of the Indian leaders. In 1929 when the Simon Commission visited Kohima, Nagas demanded that they should be excluded from the purview of Reforms and in the event of British leaving India they would like to be independent. The same Naga Club was converted into "Naga Hills District Tribal Council" in 1945 by the initiative of Charles Pawsey, the then Deputy Commissioner of Naga Hills. In 1946 the institution was renamed Naga National Council under the influence of Mr. Phizo.

It is quite surprising to note that the response of the mizos to British overtures was not much encouraging. Same Mizos raised a demand for representation in the Legislative Assembly of Assam in 1937. The movement was quickly suppressed. Thereafter during the second Great War Mr. McCall, Superintendent of Lushai Hills, tried to set up a district Chiefs' Durbar. His successor Mr. Macdonald attempted to form a District Conference consisting of 20 representatives of the chief and 20 representatives of the common people.[26] Though the conference was under the complete influence of the British Superintendent, it had not yet organized itself into an anti-Indian organ of the Lushais.

The Garos and Khasi-Jaintias came in contact with the British first and they were exposed to "exploitation" by the plains people at first. Yet we find that the tribes of these hill areas reacted against the British first and had begun to respond to the reformist movements in Shillong. After the transfer of the capital of the Assam Administration to Shillong a lot of plains people settled down there and the Brahmo Samaj and Ramakrishna Mission had received support and adherence of tribal people. But with the spread of the gospel of Christ and Government encouragement to form tribal organizations to protect their interest a change in attitude is found.

The Jaintia Durbar established in 1900 as a socio-cultural organization changed its outlook and assumed a political character.[27] To protect the interests of the Khasi tribes a Khasi States Federation was also set up.[28] Naturally the activists of these organizations made the people aware of their separate identity and interest and when the Simon Commission visited the State capital anti-congress riots shook Shillong.[29]

The Missionaries converted many tribes to Christianity and made them aliens in their own land. Some persons were given high offices and honours estensibly to impress upon the rest the result of cooperation and obedience and loyalty to the rulers. In some hills the proselytization was complete; in others some continued to worship their ancestral deities. The followers of ancestral religions were said to be animists. Those who fell under the spell of Christianity had the privilege of elementary English education and were made anti-Hindu and anti-Indian.

A contributor to *Tribal Awakening* observed: " With the establishment of the British Administration the long seclusion and isolation of the various tribal communities was coming to an end. The British broke down the barrier of separation between the tribes and the rest of India with the result that economic, administrative and other relations were opened between the tribals and non-tribals.[30]

Further the hill people who had been sub-divided into hill tribes and scheduled tribes and castes were patronized to alienate them from the caste Hindus. When the Assam Chief Commissionership was restored in 1912 in the Legislature Council seats were reserved for the Backward and Tribal communities; Reforms of 1919 and 1935 perpetuated the practice. Reservation was made for appoinment of so-called backward classes in Government services now. Not content with these provisions the Government kept the tribal areas under its immediate control without giving the ministers the charge of these people. A Government which did not undertake to administer the tribal areas directly and properly for saving revenue now kept these areas under their control in the name of protection and development. But the real motive behind the steps began to be clear when the Political Officers and District Administrators of the Hill Districts proposed before the Reforms of 1935 creation of governing areas and State for the tribes; and when at Oxford R. Coupland[31] suggested the scheme of a "Crown Colony" comprising the Hill Districts of Assam and Burma and the Frontier Tracts of Assam for British obligation towards the tribes people scented mischief.

Thus a close analysis of the impact of the British rule shows the stark and awkard facts that the seeds of communal discord and separative ethnic consciousness were disseminated by the British Administrators in Assam. At the time of withdrawal of the British the North-Eastern India was left in a flux. The different ethnic, religious, linguistic and socio-cultural communities had become conscious of their separate identity and interest. The seeds of jealousy, discord and distrust, sown through education and administrative measures, began to germinate in independent India and movements for disintegration of North-Eastern India into ethnic and linguistic divisions set afoot. Our politicians acting narrowly and selfishly and administrators short sightedly and inefficiently lead the divisive forces to their logical conclusion

NOTES

1. *Procedings of the Assam Legislative Council*, 1911-1920.
2. H. K. Barpuzan, *Op. Cit.* p. 264
3. ?
4. *Proceedings of Goverment of India*, Home Pub) Nos. 159-73, 1973
5. *Ibid.*
6. *Ibid.*
7. Reconstitution of Bengal Papers; *Proceedings of Governmen of India*, Nos. 157-67, 1905.
8. *Ibid.*
9. *Ibid.*
10. *Ibid.*
11. *Ibid.*
12. *Ibid.*
13. H. K. Barpuzan (ed), *Political History of Assam*, Gauhati, 1978, pp. 198-206.
14. *Ibid.*
15. *Ibid.*
16. For rise of Muslim Consciousness, See "Muslims as a distinct factor in Assam-Politics (1826-1947)" by DR. A. D. published in the *Journal of Historical Research*, Dibrugarh University, Vol. III, 1978.
17. *Census Report, 1941*
18. Report of the Line committee, 1937.
19. Memorandum of the Ahom Association, 29 July
20. *Ibid.*

21. *Political Consultation.*
22. *Census Report, 1931.*
23. *Proceedings of the Government of India (Foreign and Secret)* Nos. 37-39,1871.
24. "Evolution of Naga Politics", Dr. M. Aram a member of Naga Peace Mission. paper presented by Dr. M. Aram in a Seminar on Nagaland held at Shillong on November 21. 1969. under the auspices of Shillong Political Science Association.
25. S. K. Chanbe *Hill Politics in North East India.*
26. *Ibid.*
27. *Ibid.*
28. *Report of the Simon Commission.*
29. *Tribal Awakening*
30. *Conpland,* Future of India: Report on the Constitutional Problems in India, pp. 164-85.

Epilogue

Situated in the North-East corner of india and isolated from the rest of the country except through the window to Bengal, Assam through 122 years of British rule developed into a small province. No other province of India presented such diversified physical features and climatic peculiarities as did Assam in British Indian Empire. The home of myriad tribes and races, Assam accommodated Indo-Mongoloids, Indo-Aryans, Austro-Asiatics and even Negrito people. Languages of Aryan, Tibetan, Austric and even Chinese family were spoken in this province.

The British penetration into the Ahom kingdom in 1826 resulted in the gradual annexation of the contiguous territories of native princes and hill tribes. The Ahom kingdom was submerged in the overwhelming territories of the Lushai, Naga, Garo, Khasi , Jaintia and sundry tribes of North-East Frontier which were attached to it. If by Assam we mean a province where those who speak Assamese live application of the name of Assam to the new province of British India seemed quite paradoxical.

The population of Assam which was considerably thinned by the internal wars and external aggressions, at the close of the Ahom period, was increased considerably by the immigration of different races from different parts of India. With the establishment of British rule, Bengali office employees from Bengal came to serve the new Government; the people of Rajasthan came to the new economic environment to trade in the British province; labourers were imported to serve in the plantation and mining industries; people of Nepal found in Assam good grazing grounds and market for their dairy products. The population of the province increased by the addition of the neighbouring hills and plains were thus further swelled by immigration.

The socio-cultural profiles of Ahom Assam underwent considerable changes. The development of the Administration in Assam and establishment of industries brought about fundamental changes in the Assamese society. Towns and Bazars sprang up throughout the length and breadth of the country. The Assamese society which was homogeneous and vertical in strucuture now became heterogeneous in composition and parallel in style. Birth and caste which determined office and status and conferred social privilege and distinction now no longer conferred any right to office, position, distinction; postal and telegraph services, cinemas and theatres widened the outlook of the people. Society in British Assam was cosmopolitan in composition and catholic in outlook.

The new society of Assam upheld a variegated pattern of culture. Towns and bazars built with brick, mortar, sand, cement, wood and iron with sanitary and water fittings presented a new look. Centring round the new urban areas people now took to new modes of living, social gatherings, festivals, and recreations. Life had now more diversions and comforts.

Nevertheless in the new environment of socio-economic-culture percolated fissiparous forces of discord and antagonism which rent the society into segments and prepared people for a struggle of political division in the post-independent period.

The population of Assam in the British period was a conglomeration of diverse people with a separate culture and heritage. As a result of new education and environmental development however, the diverse people of India were politically united to fight against the alien rule. An Indianism not opposed to local variation and quite in harmony with regionalism had tended to develop. In Assam the diverse social interests formed themselves into organizations to further their class or community interest exclusive of national interest and received encouragement from the Government.

The economy of Assam revolutionized by Imperialism did not benefit the Assamese directly. The benefits were reaped by the British merchants who had come from outside Assam, and clerical and inconsequential technical jobs were monopolized by the Bengalis. Even the labour class was cent per cent non-Assamese. The landed property was the only means practically at the disposal of the local people with which they could procure modern amenities, comforts and recreations. When land no more could provide all that aspired for by the people, economy forced the people to look for opportunities elsewhere. But other economic opportunities and social positions had already been appropriated by non-Assamese people. The development of education and research had extended the horizons of knowledge and once the backward sections became aware of past social inequality they claimed a better status. Community within community began to be created when the Government posed as friends of the depressed communities and provided special facilities and safeguards for them.

The Government administrative measures roused jeolousies and ethnic consciousness and antagonism among people. The addition of Bengali-speaking territories to Assam compelled people of both the communities to prove their separate identity and socio-cultural differences. The same logic was applied in later phases by the tribal people under the influence of western culture to prove their distinction and separateness from the plains people.

The political parties in North-East India could not unite all the sections of the people and launch a united movement for national liberation. In fact all geographical areas and races and communities had not received new education equally and were not economically well off. Naturally their responses to national overtures differed. Moreover Government sympathy for the depressed sections held them aloof from political leaders who were held as caste Hindu exploiters.

The investigation carried on by the present project had limitation of time, resource and personnel. Therefore, the result is not up to the mark. The nature of the work has been exploratory rather than research based. But the findings, it may be held, are substantive. If further investigation is carried on each of the items spelt out in this work, more unknown factors of social dynamics may emerge and give us directions in which priority for development should be given for removing regional imbalances and eradicate social tensions.

Bibliography

Unpublished Archival Sources

Assam State Archives, Gauhati and Shillong.
Foreign Proceedings, 1876-1937.
General Department Proceedings, 1874-1937.
Judicial Department Proceedings, 1874-1935.
Revenue Department Proceedings, 1874-1935.
National Archives, New Delhi.
Foreign Political Proceedings of Government of India, 1874-1915.
Home Establishment Proceedings of Government of India, 1984-1922.
Home Public Proceedings of Government of India, 1864-1922.
Revenue Proceedings of Government of India, 1874-1940.
Reforms Department Proceedings, General Deposit, 1920.
West Bengal State Archives, Calcutta.
Judicial Proceedings, 1854-1905.
General Proceedings, 1854-1905.
Police Proceedings, 1860-1905.

Published Government Reports ands Gazetteers

Abstract of Intelligence Report, Assam Police, 1874-1904, 1912-1940.
Abstract of Intelligence Report, Eastern Bengal of Assam Police, 1905-1912.
Addresses presented to Lord Curzon, Shillong, 1900.

An Account of Assam and its Administration, Shillong, 1903.
Assam District Gazetteers, 1906.
Assam Administration Reports, 1874-76 -1904, 1912-1944.
Census of India Reports, 1881-1951.
Eastern Bengal and Assam Administration Reports, 1905-1911..
Proceedings of the Assam legislative Assembly, 1912-1946.
Report on the Working of the Assam Legislative Assembly, 1942.
Report of A.J.M. Mill on Assam, 1854.
Report of the Indian Constitution of Reforms,1919.
Report on the Indian Statutory Commission, Vols.I.II, 1929.
Report of the Line Committee, 1937.

Books

Amanatulla, A. : *A History of Cooch Behar, Cooch Behar, 1936*

Archaryya, N.N.: *History of Medeaival Assam, Gauhati, 1966.*

Bailey, F.M.: *China-Tibet-Assam,* London, 1945.

Bardoloi,K.C.(ed) : *Sadar Aminar Atma Jivani*, North-Gauhati, 1960.

Barpuzari, H.K. : *Political History of Assam*, Vol. I, Gauhati, 1977.

Bucchanon-Hamilton,F: *Account of Assam 1807-14*, Calcutta

Baruah, H.N.: *Asamor Samasya Aru Bhabisat* (in Assamese).

Baruah, K.L : *Early History of Kamrupa*. Gauhati, 1945.

Baruah, B.K.: *A Cultural History of Assam*, Gauhati, 1969.

Basu, N.K.: *Assam in the Ahom Age*, Calcutta 1965.

Bhuyan, S.K.: *Anglo-Assamese Relations, 1771-1826*, Gauhati,1949.

Bose, M.L.: *Historical and Constitutional Developments of North East India*, New Delhi, 1979.

Chaube, S.K.: *Hill Politics in North-East India*, Orient Longman, 1973.

Coupland, R.: *The Future of India: Report on the constitutional Problems in India,* London, 1943.

Das. H.P.: *Geography of Assam*, NBT, 1970.

Dutta, K.N.: *Land marks of Freedom Struggle in Assam*, Gauhati, 1969.

Dube, S.M.(ed.): *North-East India*, New Delhi, 1977.

Dalton, E.T.: *Descripive Ethnology of Bengal*, 1905.

Gait, E.: *History of Assam*, Calcutta, 1905.

Goswami, P.C.: *Economic Development of Assam*, Bombay, 1963.

Guha, A.: *Planter Raj to Swaraj*, New Delhi, 1976.

Greirson : *Linguistic Survey of India*, Vol.III Calcutta,1907.

Hunter, W.W.: *A Statistical Account of Assam*, Vol, I-II. Reprint, Imperial Gazetteer, Vols IV ,VI.

Kakati, B.K. : *Mother Goddess Kamakshya*, Gauhati 1948, *Assamese its formation and development*, Gauhati, 1941.

Lahiri, R.M. : *Annexation of Assam*, Calcutta, 1954.

Mackenzie, A : *History of the Relations of the Government with the Hill Tribes of the North-East Frontier of Bengal*, Calcutta, 1884.

Majumdar, R.C.(ed) : *British Paramountcy and Indian Renaissance,* Vol, X, Bombay, 1965.

M'Cosh, J. N. : *Topography of Assam*, Calcutta, 1837

Neog, D, : *New Light on the History of Asamiya Literature,* Gauhati, 1962

Palande, M. R. : *Indian Administration*, London, 1947.

Pemberton, R. B. : *Report on the Eastern Frontier of Bengal*, Calcutta, 1835.

Robinson W. : *A Descriptive Account of Assam*, Calcutta, 1841.

Rao, V. V. : *Local Self Government*, Gauhatim, 1973.

Regmi, D. R. : *Modern Nepal*, Vol. II, Calcutta, 1975.

Reid, R. : *History of Frontier Areas Bordering* on Assam from 1883-1941, Shillong, 1942.

Ray-Burma, B. K. & : Thakuria, S. P. : *Demographic and Socio-Economic Profiles of North-East India,* New Delhi, 1961.

Saikia, C. P. : *Lokshminath Bezaruah,* Gauhati, 194

Shakespeare, W. : *History of the Assam Rifles*, London, 1929.

Vasu N. N. : *Social History of Kamrupa,* Calcutta, 1922

Verrier, Elwin : *India's North-East Frontier,* London, 1959.
A Philosophy for NEFA, Shillong, 1957.
Wright, D. (ed). : *History of Nepal*, Calcutta, 1877.

Journals

Journals of Assam Political Science Association, 1976
North-Eastern Research Bulletin, Dibrugarh University, 1967-1977
Shodhak, Jaipur, 1969-1977
Tribal Awakening, published by the Christian Institute for the Study of Religion and Society, Bangalore, 1965.

Index